jil eaton's KNITTING SCHOOL

jil eaton's KNITTING SCHOOL

the complete guide to becoming a confident knitter

POTTER CRAFT
New York

Published in the United States by Potter Craft, an imprint of the Crown Publishing Group,
a division of Random House, Inc., New York.
www.crownpublishing.com
www.pottercraft.com

Library of Congress Cataloging-in-Publication Data
Eaton, Jil, 1949-
Jil Eaton's knitting school : the complete guide to becoming a confident knitter / Jil Eaton ;
photographs by Nina Fuller. – 1st ed.
p. cm.
Includes bibliographical references and index.
ISBN 978-0-307-58647-6
1. Knitting. I. Title.
TT820.E2545 2010
746.43'2–dc22
2010000477

Printed in China

Design by Beth St. James
Photography by Nina Fuller
Photography Art Direction by Jil Eaton
Styling by Merle Hagelin, Jil Eaton, Mark Dube
Pattern Design by Jil Eaton
Drawings by Jil Eaton
Technical Illustrations by Joni Coniglio
Technical Writing and Editing by Stephanie Doben
Pattern Checking by Janice Bye

10 9 8 7 6 5 4 3 2 1

First Edition

MinnowKnits™ patterns and books and yarns are distributed by
Classic Elite Yarns, 125 Western Avenue, Lowell, MA 01851 www.classiceliteyarns.com

www.minnowknits.com
www.classiceliteyarns.com
www.ninafuller.net

dedication

..... to my toast band mates, Kathleen Egan, Ted Arnold, and Tori Lambert, who have given me so many joyous hours over the past years, full of fun and harmony, the perfect prescription for health and happiness and creativity—thanks for every single note!

contents

knit

Knit: Pronunciation:(nit)

Verb: knit or knit-ted; knit-ing

From the Middle English knitten, from the Old English cnyttan, like the Old English cnotta knot, from the Proto-Germanic knuttjan, and the Old Norse knyta.

Transitive verb: to tie together; to link firmly and closely; to form a textile yarn in a series of connected loops with needles or machine

Intransitive verb: to make knitted textiles or objects; to become compact. To grow together as in bones, to become drawn together as a close-knit group.

Noun: knitter; a piece of knitting.

Ah, knitting! I love the fact that knitting is an “ing” word, alive, happening, and ongoing. What wonders we can create with just two sticks and a string. It’s amazing and quite magical as we watch our knitted garment evolve, transforming from a series of simple cast-on stitches to a beautiful, fully-formed fabric. Knitting provides a plethora of happiness, both for those who spend all the pleasant hours with needles in hand, and for those who receive the lovingly hand-knit delights at a birthday party or other holiday event. Historically, hand-knit garments have been found as far back as ancient Egypt. Through the ages techniques have expanded and evolved, but the basic form of interlocked loops has remained the same. In times past there was always an older generation of very experienced knitters on hand to help the novices. As that is not always the case in our very busy and technologically-saturated world, this *Knitting School* collection is designed to teach you to knit or to encourage you to return to knitting and to help you refine your skills. The collection provides eighteen projects in an ever-expanding technical sequence. My signature QuickKnits™ are designed for instant gratification, chic but simply made, with charming details providing that *je ne sais quoi* factor. And this collection includes more fashion-forward garments as well. There are myriad techniques for knitting, and I have chosen my favorites, sharing my tips and tricks for perfect knitting. Do enjoy this collection; if you knit every project, even as a true beginner you will have mastered the craft with aplomb.

Remember, when we’re knitting all is right with the world!

Jil Eaton
Portland, Maine
August 2009

about this book

After writing my "Ask Jil" column in *Knit Simple* magazine, I realized that many of my readers are beginners who could benefit from a few knitting lessons. With that in mind, I've designed this book as a series of workshops, where techniques are learned step by step, building on skills as you go. Patterns follow the lessons, giving you the opportunity to practice your new techniques, and the chapters are organized according to ability levels, so you can easily advance at your own pace. You begin with the simplest garter-stitch scarf, and then you learn the purl stitch, the basic stockinette stitch, the seed stitch, felting, embroidery, Fair Isle, stripes, pleats, cables, and even lace and multistitch patterns.

Many projects are my signature QuickKnits™, but this collection also includes more chic and fitted garments in smaller gauges. There are projects for everyone—mom, dad, babies, children, and even the family dog. I've also included many of my favorite knitting tips, which you'll find sprinkled throughout the chapters. The tips will help you navigate the knitting process more easily. When you are just beginning to knit, it's challenging to find the right way to hold the needles and keep your tension even, but if you persevere you'll soon find that knitting has become second nature to you.

I learned to knit from my beautiful mother at the age of four, and I haven't stopped since. Knitting gives me endless pleasures, is a comfort in difficult times, and is an almost a Zen-like meditative activity.

knitting basics

What does it take to become a confident knitter? I believe in investing in the best tools you can find, ones you will use for many years to come. Knitting is a constant delight and I encourage you to set yourself up the right way at the beginning. Check out your local yarn shops and the Internet for the items described here.

The Perfect Knitting Kit

A small, clear, zippered case, such as a cosmetics bag, is perfect for holding all your knitting paraphernalia because you can see inside to find the tools you need. Having a portable kit allows you to take it with you on whatever project you are knitting. Find a case that gives you pleasure because it will become the backbone of your knitting life; my case is from Agnès b, discovered on a trip to Paris.

Small, very sharp scissors, for yarn use only.

Needle size/gauge ruler. For those with an iPhone, there is now an app for needle sizing!

Retractable measuring tape.

Yarn T-pins and **yarn safety pins** for pinning and marking.

Small calculator—essential for changing gauges.

Stitch holders, both long and short. Coated metal English Aeros are always in my case; plastic Japanese holders that open at either end work well, too.

Dentists' tool, with one hooked end and one smooth end, is invaluable for working out knots, picking up dropped stitches, and undoing sticky yarns. You can use it any time you would use a crochet hook—only it's easier.

Crochet hooks, one large and one small, such as a D and a K.

Stitch markers. Split-rings are good as they are easily moved or removed.

Tapestry or yarn needles. I prefer the Japanese Chibi needles with bent tips; they come in lovely little plastic cases.

Cable needles. I recommend straight cable needles, sizes 3, 6 and 10 U.S., in bamboo or wood.

Point protectors, both large and small, to keep your work on the needles.

Pen and small notebook, for notations, row counting, and design ideas.

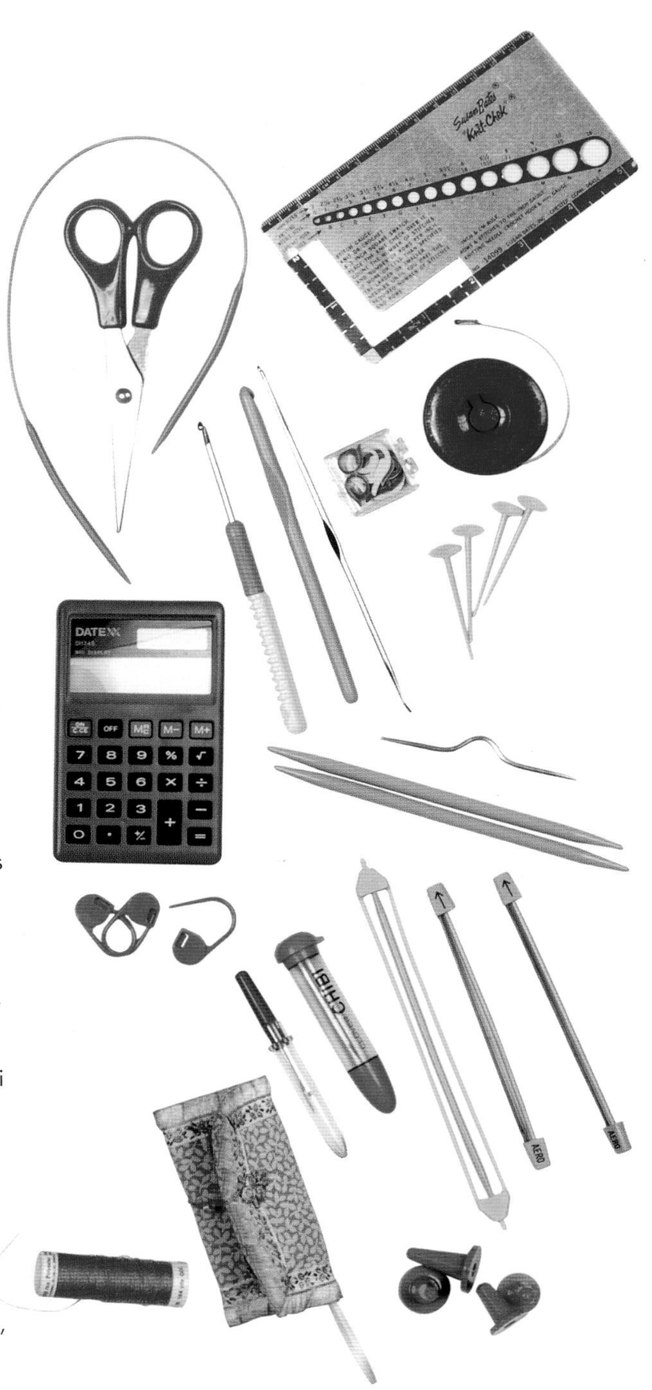

Needles

Often beginning knitters will buy only the needles they need for their current project, but I guarantee that you will, *sans doute*, eventually want a complete set of needles, including doubles in your favorite sizes. So why not invest at the beginning? There are also needle kits, available in metal from Boyle and in plastic from Denise, that have interchangeable cords and needle tips that clip or screw together, providing you with circular needles in many needle sizes and lengths. You will also need cases for straight, double-pointed, and circular needles.

Needles come in various materials and most knitters find that different needles work better for different projects, depending on the yarn or pattern. Basic needles are available in coated metal, casein, plastic, bamboo, and wood. I love the old-fashioned plastic needles for most projects; they are soft and warm in your hands, and quiet as you knit. I like double-pointed needles in bamboo or wood for knitting in the round, because they are less slippery than metal types. Addi Turbos are best for circular knitting, and they really do speed up your knitting time.

Straight needles, available in many materials, must be flawlessly smooth and have points that are well shaped. Always use needles that are no longer than 14 inches (35.5cm); anything longer will put stress on your wrists. You can use circular needles for larger projects, working back and forth instead of in the round. You can also use straight needles with plastic extensions for larger projects and for travel knitting; they have no pesky needle ends to bother a companion.

Circular needles are needle tips connected by a thin plastic cable. Circular needles are used for knitting in the round, and for working back and forth on larger projects. Addi Turbo circular knitting needles, made of silver plated brass, are lovely to work with and they really can speed up your knitting time. Make sure the

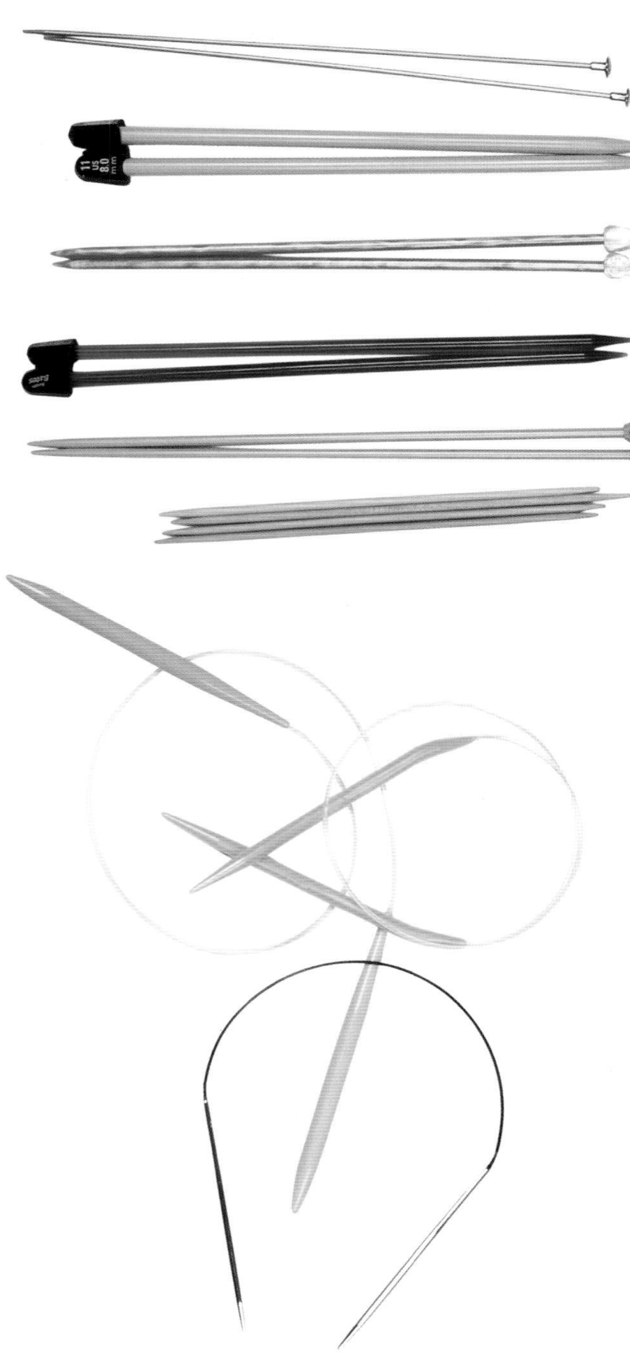

length of the circular needle is the correct size for your project. It must be smaller than the circumference of the knitting.

Double-pointed needles, called "dpns," are used for knitting in the round when you work on small sizes and are always used for I-cord. I use bamboo dpns; they are light and stay in place as you rotate your work. I always carry a few in my knitting kit, too, to use for emergency repair and as temporary stitch holders.

Needle Cases

Needle cases are wonderful for organizing your needles. Cases for both straight and circular needles are available in several styles and sizes. I use school pencil cases to hold my dpns, which works very well. Keeping your tools and needles well organized can only add to your knitting pleasure.

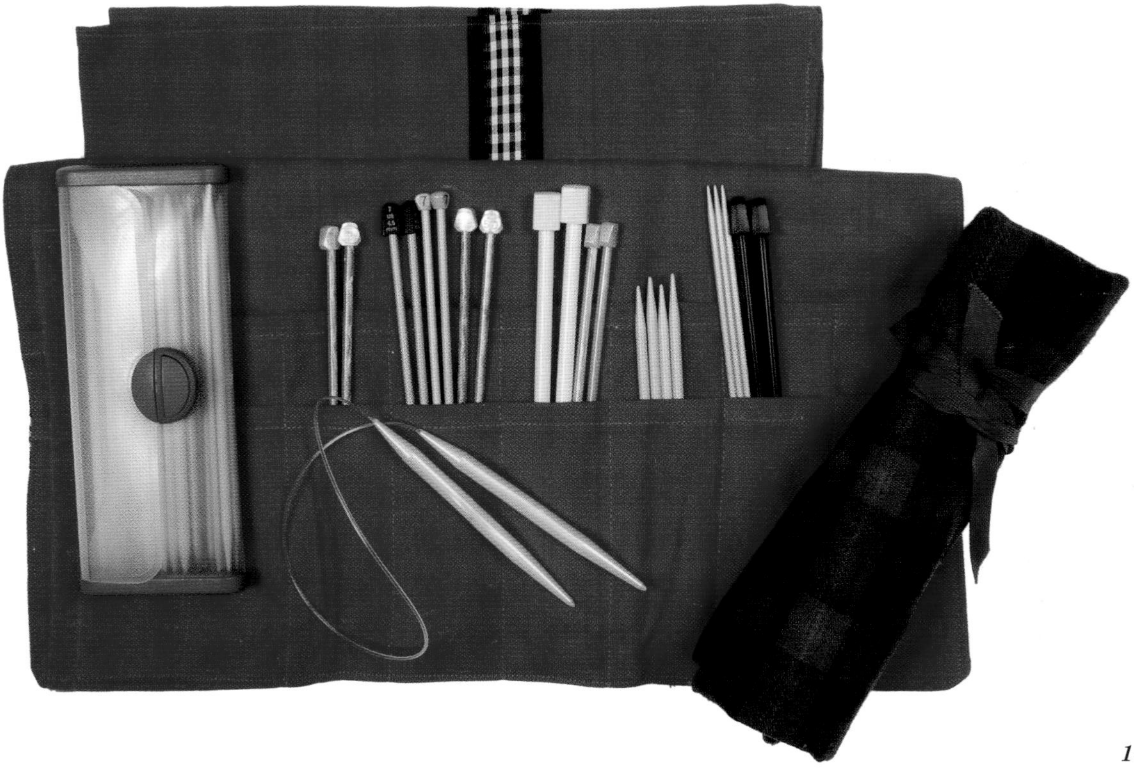

Other Knitting Equipment

The following items will help make your knitting easier and more organized.

Baskets, bags, and containers

I have many, many baskets and bags, in all shapes and sizes, including lightweight versions for traveling and stackable milk crates for organizing yarn in my studio. There are several clever variations available in knitting shops; one I saw recently was made of lightweight, colorful rip-stop nylon that converts into a backpack. Investigate the possibilities, and discover what works best for you. I always like to have more than one project in the works, one for easy, fast knitting, others for more complex and challenging stitching. You can simply move your trusty knitting kit from one container to the other as you switch projects.

Knitting notebook

I require that all my students keep a three-ring binder filled with clear insert pages that open at the top to organize individual projects. Slip the pattern or your personal photocopy with any notes or comments, a small amount of the yarn used for the project, and the gauge swatch for reference. The yarn is perfect for any later repairs, and the notebook becomes an on-going history of your projects. I always include the date and the name of the lucky recipient.

Jil's tip

If you have an idea, jot it down so it doesn't disappear!

PHOTOCOPYING PATTERNS

The only time it is ever legal to copy a pattern for distribution is if the pattern clearly states that it is in the public domain; otherwise a copyright is in effect even if it not printed on the pattern. You can, of course, make a single copy for your own use.

Yarn winder

A table-mounted yarn winder is not a necessity, but it is a great timesaving tool. Yarn that comes in hanks must be rolled into balls before you begin to knit. Of course, some of us love that yarn-winding ritual—I have sweet memories of helping my mother wind up her yarn, but now I must say I love my yarn winder. Winders can be found in knitting shops, in knitting catalogs, or on the Internet.

Knitting lights

Good light is absolutely essential for good knitting. Period. A high-intensity, adjustable light will help prevent mistakes in your handwork, saving you from problems later, and from lost time. A directed light will not annoy others in the room, but will keep your knitting well lit. I keep these lights in every room in my house, as well as in my studio.

About Yarn

The selection of yarns on the market today is amazing and, to me, tantalizing and addictive. Technology and machinery have made it possible to both invent delicious new fibers and blends and make improvements on the basic ones. The yarn is the essence of your project. After the knitting is finished, the garment will retain the qualities of the yarn itself. I always recommend purchasing the very best yarn you can afford because the better the quality of the yarn, the better the look of the finished garment. A complex sweater worked in a poor quality synthetic will be a disappointment, no matter how beautifully it is knit.

Wool, the favorite hand-knitting yarn in the world, is soft and cozy, wears well, and has a long useable life. Wool comes from sheep, is warm and elastic, and has insulating properties. Wool yarn is made up of strands of fiber called plies. Plies may be single, or doubled or tripled and twisted together. There are various grades of wool so look for the finer ones such as Merino, which come from sheep with exceptionally long, soft coats.

Cotton, an ancient fiber that is grown in warmer climates all over the world, is another fabulous fiber. It takes dye beautifully, is washable, is appropriate for those living in warmer climates, and can be worn by anyone with allergies. Cotton yarn is usually quite smooth, so stitch definition is easily visible. It does not have the stretch and give of wool, making it a bit harder to knit with, and it can be unforgiving if you make a mistake. Mercerized cottons are treated with a solution and then stretched for smoother, more lustrous, longwearing, and pill- and shrink-resistant finish.

Linen yarn is strong and lustrous, and comes from the stems of the flax plant. Like cotton, linen is washable and is delightful to wear in hot climates. Linen is a heavy fiber, and is usually spun in lighter, finer weights.

Mixed fiber blends such as wool with cotton, cotton with silk, or one of these with a synthetic, are another knitting option. I always prefer the natural fiber blends, both to hold in my hands as I knit and to wear.

Mohair comes from Angora goats. The animals used for the fiber originally came from Ankara (modern-day Turkey), but Texas has become a big producer of mohair. Mohair is light and airy, very warm, and perfect for chic outerwear. Even though the mohair fiber seems very light, it knits up quickly in a bulky gauge. Kid mohair comes from baby angora goats, and is much softer and finer than regular mohair. I think mohair is often misunderstood in the United States, as it is really too warm for indoor wear. Try mohair for an outdoor jacket and I think you'll be pleasantly surprised.

Angora comes from Angora rabbits, and is gorgeous. The fibers are very short, resulting in the fiber's tendency to shed. The best quality angora is combed from the rabbits rather than sheared, and is less likely to have the shedding problem. Angora is my favorite fiber for luxury baby layettes.

Silk yarn comes from silk worms and is very expensive because the harvesting process is difficult. Silk is very strong, but can be susceptible to fading.

Bamboo yarns have been developed as a result of environmental consciousness — bamboo replenishes itself easily — and the resulting fiber is soft and pliant, lovely to knit with. Bamboo is very nice for baby layette garments.

Standard yarn weight system

Yarn Weight Category & Symbol	0 LACE	1 SUPER FINE	2 FINE	3 LIGHT	4 MEDIUM	5 BULKY	6 SUPER BULKY
Types of Yarn	Fingering, 10-count crochet thread	Sock, Fingering, Baby	Sport, Baby	DK, Light Worsted	Worsted, Afghan, Aran	Chunky, Craft, Rug	Bulky, Roving
Knit Gauge Range (in Stockinette Stitch to 4 inches	33–40 sts	27–32 sts	23–26 sts	21–24 st	16–20 sts	12–15 sts	6–11 sts
Recommended Needle Size (Metric)	1.5–2.25 mm	2.25–3.25 mm	3.25–3.75 mm	3.75–4.5 mm	4.5–5.5 mm	5.5–8 mm	8 mm and larger
Recommended Needle Size (U.S.)	000–1	1 to 3	3 to 5	5 to 7	7 to 9	9 to 11	11 and larger

Adapted from the Standard Yarn Weight System of the Craft Yarn Council of America.

Alpaca comes from animals that are members of the South American camel family, and the fleece is spun into lovely soft, lustrous, warm yarn. I love alpaca for boot socks. It's also perfect for cozy snow boots or winter sports.

Cashmere comes from goats in China and Tibet, and is *la crème de la crème* of yarns, with a very low micron count resulting in a very fine fiber. (Micron count is the diameter of the fiber; one micron is equal to 1/25400 of an inch or one millionth of a meter!) It takes dyes beautifully and is a dream to knit with.

HOW MANY SKEINS?

How do you figure out how many skeins of yarn to buy? It just takes a little math. Divide the number of yards in one skein into the total number of yards needed for the project, and round up. For example, if the project calls for 1,440 yards and the yarn you are using comes in 77-yard skeins, divide 1,440 by 77 to get 18.70. Round up to 19 and add one for a little insurance. You will need twenty skeins of yarn.

Yarn Buying Guide

Finding the right yarn for your projects is part of the creative fun of knitting, so visit your local yarn shop and devote some time to perusing the yarn. Touching the skeins, searching for colors, and discovering new color combinations is all part of your knitting experience. If you have any questions about a particular yarn, buy one skein so you can knit a swatch to make sure that yarn will work for your project the way you want it to. If it's not quite right, having one ball in your stash is much better than having ten!

I generally prefer designing with worsted or bulky weights, speeding up my trademark QuickKnit™ process, but sometimes a double knitting or sportweight is perfect. When buying yarns, always check the ball band for information such as gauge, yardage, dye lot, country of origin, fiber makeup, and washing instructions. Yarns come either in pre-wound balls or in hanks; hanks must be wound into balls before knitting. Buy enough yarn for your project plus one more ball or hank, just to make sure you have enough. Yarn shops will usually let you return any unused balls, and it would be unfortunate if you were to run out only to find the yarn had been discontinued.

Again, always look for the highest quality yarns you can find. When I was growing up in Maine you could only find sturdy, scratchy Maine wool. Now we have an explosion of fabulous fibers to choose from. The Internet is a great resource for yarns; it's an especially good source if you know your fibers. You can trust any of the companies featured in this book, too, for always providing yarns that are in the top tier.

Always Knitting to Fit

Anyone who has been in one of my classes will know that my mantra is gauge, gauge, gauge! Getting the gauge is the single most important step in knitting.

The gauge is the number of stitches and rows per inch; the gauge swatch is a four-inch (10-centimeter) square, knit in the pattern stitch using the recommended needle size, or the size necessary to get that gauge. Getting the correct gauge allows you to make a fabric that is even and smooth, with the right drape and hand, resulting in the accurate measurements for the garment.

Knitting at even a half stitch off gauge will make a significant difference in the final measurement of your garment. For instance, if the pattern calls for one hundred stitches at five stitches per inch, and you are getting five and a half stitches to the inch, your sweater will measure eighteen inches instead of twenty. Two inches is a lot on any project, and can make the difference between a beautiful garment and an ill-fitting one. Why avoid a few minutes of knitting the swatch when not doing so may mean that hours and hours of work may be incorrect?

I know many knitters skip knitting the gauge swatch, assuming they will knit to gauge. But taking the time to stitch a swatch will make all the difference in the success of your knitting. As Nike says, "Just do it!" Make a habit of knitting your gauge swatch and you will be a better knitter for life.

To begin your swatch use the needles suggested in the pattern, and remember they are just that — a suggestion. Cast on the number of stitches necessary to make a 4-inch (10cm) swatch, plus six stitches for a border of three garter stitches at the beginning and end of every row. Knit three rows. Then work in the pattern called for until the piece measures 4 inches

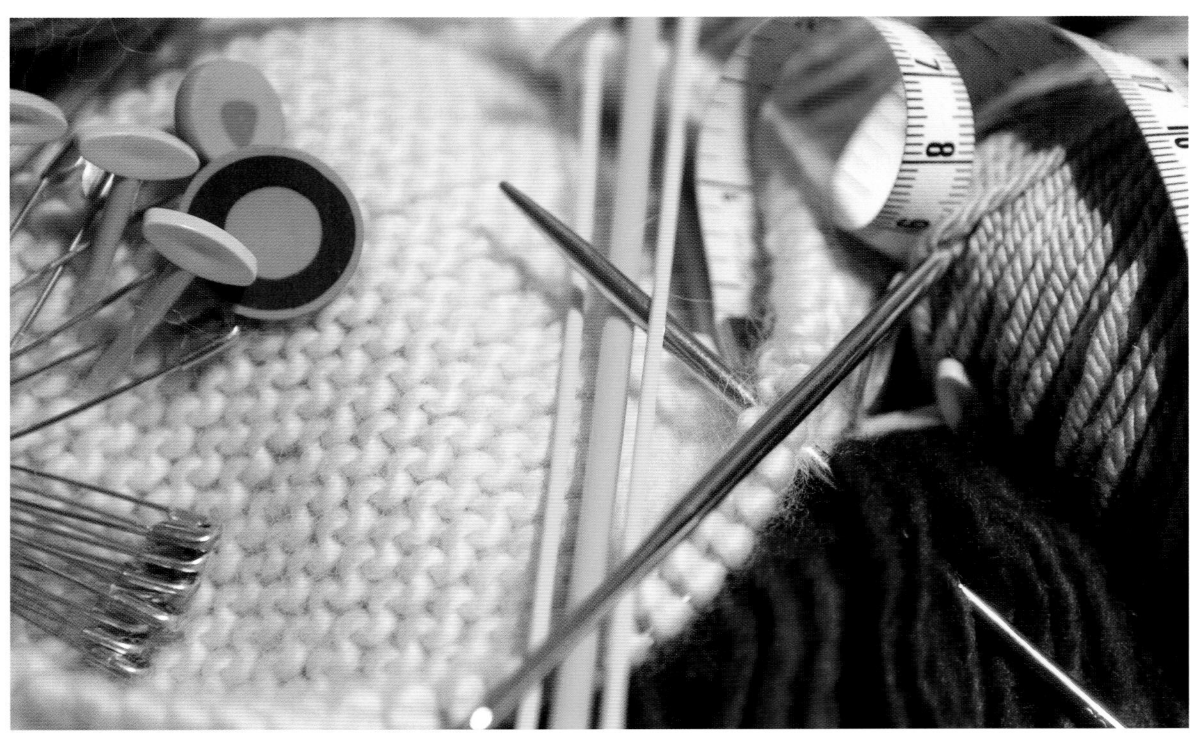

(10cm) from the beginning of the pattern, then knit three rows and bind off. Lay the swatch on a flat, smooth surface. Measure inside the garter stitch frame; it should measure 4 inches (10cm) exactly. If your swatch is too big, or if you have too few stitches per inch (centimeter), change to needles one size smaller, and repeat the process. If your swatch is too small, or there are too many stitches per inch, switch to the next larger size needles. Change one needle size either up or down at a time and keep knitting swatches until you get the correct gauge.

As you knit more you will begin to know your knitting style. I start my swatch one needle size down from the recommended size because I knit fast and loose. The number of stitches per inch or centimeter is the most important. If the row gauge is eluding you, you can adjust as you work through the pattern—a good reason to buy extra yarn. We all knit differently with different needles and yarns. Always work your gauge swatch with the same needles you will be using for the project because there can be a difference in gauge among plastic, metal, and bamboo needles on the same yarn.

Jil's Tip
Measure your swatch after washing and blocking for the most accurate results.

The yarns used for each knitted sample in this book are listed in the patterns, so you can find the exact colors and weights. If you want to substitute yarns for any of the projects, make sure that the gauge is the same as the original. For the best fit, use yarn that is the same weight as the recommended yarn. And, again, I recommend that you always use the very best yarns you can afford.

Measuring

Choosing the correct size to knit is an important step in the success of your project. If you are making a garment for yourself, find a garment in your closet that is similar, then lay it flat to measure it. Use those figures to find the best size for your knitting project, referring to the size measurements in the pattern. My children's wear silhouette tends to be generous, with room for easy dressing and comfortable movement. Check out the measurements in the chart in the pattern. If you are knitting for a child, measure carefully, and go to the next biggest size. And remember that babies grow at an alarming rate, so keep that in mind when choosing a size for your little one.

The following is a guideline for measuring both children and adults.

Chest/bust: Measure around the fullest part of the bust/chest for adults; around the chest, just under the arms for children.

Sleeve length: Measure from the center back at the nape of the neck to the wrist, with arm outstretched.

Center back: Measure from the center of the back at the nape of the neck to the waist.

Head: Measure around the head at the widest part, across the forehead and right above the ears.

Foot length: Place the tape measure on the floor and measure from heel to longest toe.

Jil's Tip
Measure your work with a metal ruler that can't be stretched!.

When you are measuring your handwork place the pieces flat on a hard surface, and measure without pulling. Measure straight up the garment piece, ignoring garment shaping. If you need to measure a shaped edge, such as an armhole, place a metal ruler across the body at the place where the armhole shaping starts. Measure straight up from the ruler. Slight differences in length can be blocked, but if you count your rows the pieces should match exactly.

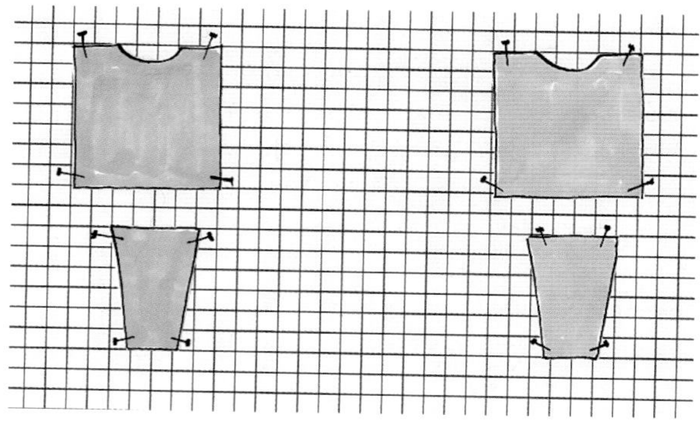

Blocking

Blocking is the process knitters use to finish the garment pieces—setting the knitting and evening out the stitches— before sewing the garment together. Blocking reduces curling, makes edges straighter, and makes finishing easier. For blocking you will need a blocking board, a wonderful invention that is padded and has a checkerboard pattern that helps you get your edges straight, and T-pins. Although a blocking board makes the blocking much easier, you can always use your ironing board, especially for smaller pieces.

Jil's Tip
Never block ribbing; it should remain stretchy.

Pin the finished pieces to the blocking board or ironing board, pinning all the edges and checking your measurements as you work. Lightly steam the pieces at the appropriate iron setting for the type of yarn you are using, holding the iron above the knitting and not letting it touch the fabric. Air dry your garment flat on a towel, mesh rack, or on the blocking board. Blocking generally improves the look of your garment, as long as it is done very gently. Some fibers, such as specialty yarns, should not be blocked, nor should knitting with trims and beads.

Laundering

You spend hours and hours knitting your wonderful hand-knits, so you want to take care when it's time to wash them. Use the care instructions on the ball band and your gauge swatch to test the washability of the yarn. Many yarns can be machine washed if you place them in a small mesh bag and use tepid water and a very gentle cycle to help them hold their shape. Use a no-rinse yarn soap such as Eucalan, which is available at fine yarn shops as well as on the Internet. These no-rinse products recommend that you soak your garments in the washing machine for about twenty minutes, then go straight to the spin cycle. Felting and shrinking happen with agitation and water temperature changes; the spin cycle simply gets all the water out. Air dry the knitted item on a mesh rack or towel. Wonderful "superwash" yarns can be machine-washed using gentle laundry soap (not the no-rinse products because they will ruin the garment). Of course, if the care instructions on the ball band say "dry clean only," then, for best results, dry clean only!

How to Read a Pattern

I began knitting at the age of four, and because I couldn't yet read I was always designing my own things (doll clothes, to be precise). As I grew older I did try to use patterns, but relied mostly on the charts and schematics, as all the words were so confusing. Over the years, I found some things that helped me become a skilled pattern reader and knitter: reading through the pattern thoroughly before beginning and using a schematic, or making my own.

Always read through your pattern completely, just as you do with a recipe. This is important because it will help you understand all the steps involved and give you a mental picture of the complete garment. It will help prevent you from gliding along, knitting several inches past the place to decrease, for example, and having to rip out. Most patterns are accompanied by a schematic, a black-and-white diagram that shows the shaping and includes measurements for each of the various parts. It really helps to refer to the schematic as you read through your pattern, and you can check against it as you proceed with your knitting.

If your pattern does not have a good schematic, get some graph paper and make your own. Begin with a line at the bottom for the cast-on stitches, and using the squares as inches, measure up to the next step. This visual aid shows the shaping, any increases or decreases, the number of inches between instructions, and all the parts of the garment. You may want to get some knitter's graph paper (available on the Internet), which is available in all gauges. With this, you can make a schematic for the size you are knitting. You can use this chart to make notes as you proceed, which will help as you knit the other front piece or the other sleeve. Read slowly, and include every step that's a change in the pattern, and you will have a fabulous working tool.

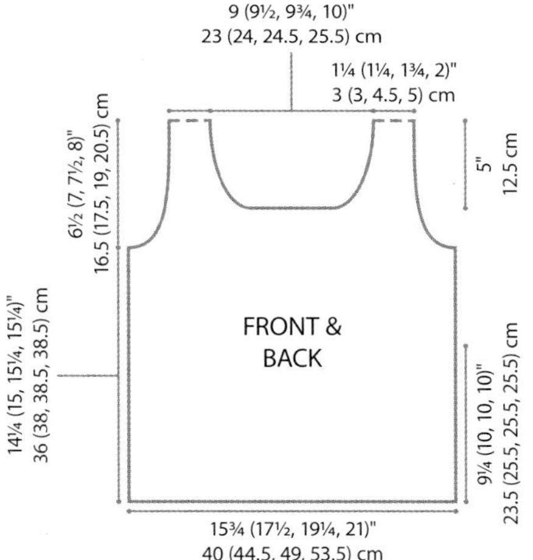

Knitting patterns can seem complex and daunting, but I have found if you simply slow down and read the pattern carefully, step by step, the design unfolds almost like magic. Heels will turn, cables will wind, Fair Isle patterns will appear, and soon your confidence will grow. Knitters know this magic, this Zen-like activity that brings us such joy, and patterns are at the heart of it. Be patient and you will succeed.

Jil's Tip

Check your gauge again after working about 4 inches (10cm) of your project just to be sure you're still getting the correct gauge.

Knitting Abbreviations

Patterns are written using American Knitting Language, with specific ways of stating various techniques. The following is a list of commonly used abbreviations.

approx	Approximately
beg	Beginning
BO	Bind off
CC	Contrasting color
CO	Cast on
cont	Continue(ing)s
cn	Cable needle
dec	Decrease(ing)
dpn	Double-pointed needle
est	Established
foll	Following
inc (s)	Increase(s)
k	Knit
k1fb	Knit one in front and back of next stitch
k2tog	Knit two stitches together
MC	Main color
p	Purl
p2tog	Purl two stitches together
pat (s)	Pattern(s)
psso	Pass slipped stitch over last stitch worked
rem	Remaining
rep	Repeat(s)
rev St st	Reverse Stockinette
rib	Rib(bing)
rnd(s)	Round(s)
RS	Right side
Sl	Slip(ed) (ping)
Ssk	Slip, slip, knit
st(s)	Stitch(es)
St st	Stockinette Stitch
Tog	Together
WS	Wrong side
YO	Yarn over

let's knit!

Knitting is a way of life. Knitters are the luckiest people on earth because they always have a wonderful way to occupy themselves, at home alone, while traveling, or with friends.

Knitting on the go

Knitters always have a project to work on, whether traveling, waiting for the bus, watching sports, or sitting at the playground. Small portable projects like socks and hats are perfect. They are small enough to be carried easily, yet ready for those twenty minutes sitting outside the dentist's office. We try not to engender knitting envy as we tote our various projects from place to place, amusing ourselves and creating beauty in the world.

Starting a knitting group

Knitters are a special kind, and in my experience we love getting together to knit, chat, and share—everything from favorite projects to child-raising stories. There is something quite extraordinary that happens when you get together with like-minded friends: you'll knit the evening away sharing not only techniques and projects, but also ideas and experiences. We shore each other up in this safe haven of clicking needles, warmth, and conversation.

Knitting groups can be open to any level of proficiency; the more experienced knitters are an inspiration for the beginners. To start a knitting group of your own, you'll want to find a suitable location and decide on an appropriate time. You might start with a few friends and let your group grow as word gets out. Find a time that works for your friends, but be flexible—you may find at your first meeting that there is interest in a different time. To accommodate students and those who work during the day, choose an evening or a weekend time.

The location is important: your meeting place should be centrally located, easily accessible, and within your budget. Local coffee shops, libraries, church halls, and schools are some venues to try. You could even check with your local yarn shop; they might be delighted to have you. Make sure you find a venue with tables; it's much nicer to have your work supported on a tabletop. And if your group is small enough, you can meet in each other's homes, rotating your schedule.

Some knitting groups have a stated purpose that helps to focus the group. If you decide to take that route, be sure to use it in your advertising and promotional materials. Learning new techniques, knitting for charity, and sharing stitches and projects are a few ideas.

To promote your knitting group, place a listing in your local newspaper's community calendar. If your town has a television station or community group with a website that promotes local activities, ask to have your meeting time and place added to the list. Newsletters for hospitals and houses of worship are also good places to advertise. Many knitters start a group on Ravelry.com or publicize it through Meetup.com. Another option is to create a flyer and distribute it around town. Keep it simple and direct, and include a fun graphic such as a ball of yarn and needles. Once your group is established collect members' email addresses and use them to keep in touch.

Group knitting is a rewarding experience! One of my friends is a part of a knitting circle that has been meeting for more than twelve years; this group has become an important and integral part of the members' lives. I'm confident that once you decide to begin a group, you'll find a knitting club will become a delightful part of your knitting life.

Knitting for charity

There are many ways you or your group can knit for local or national charities. Hospitals need preemie caps and chemo hats; homeless shelters want blankets, hats and mittens; organizations for the elderly distribute afghans and warm hats; and the Ronald MacDonald House appreciates comforting hand-knit items of all kinds. You can use up your own yarn stashes and, at the same time, give a little bit of love with every stitch!

Going on a field trip

Many knitting groups pool resources to organize fiber-related group excursions. Good destinations include local yarn shops, sheep and wool festivals, llama farms, designers' studios, and yarn companies. We all love to meet other knitters and investigate the latest in yarns and equipment. There is an ever-increasing number of conventions, retreats, classes, knit-ins, and yarn swaps taking place throughout the year. Companies often offer special sales or discounts for group visits. So save up and get going!

beginner's delights

I always take great joy in beginning a new class, and part of the fun is selecting the projects to be taught. The projects in this chapter have been designed to start off your knitting life with ease and charm. The first three all use the garter stitch, which is just knitting every row, giving you a chance to perfect this basic stitch. After you learn the second most important stitch, the purl, you will be able to make a sweater for each member of your family. When just learning to knit, be sure to knit at least a little bit every day—it will make your craft second nature and help you remember your techniques.

PROJECT INDEX

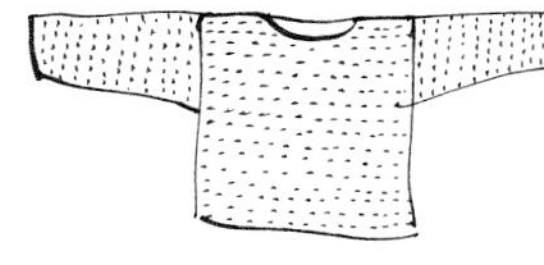

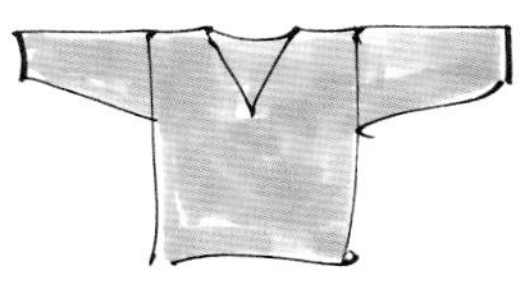

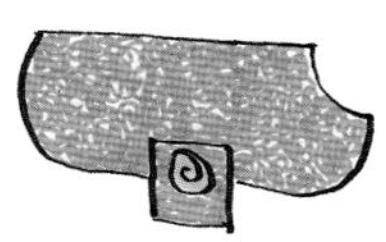

LESSON 1

1

2

How to Make a Slip Knot

You'll need to make a slip knot for the beginning of the cast-on.

1. Hold the yarn in your left hand, leaving a 6-inch (15cm) length free. Wrap the yarn from the skein into a circle and bring it from below and up through the center of the circle. Insert the needle under this strand.

2. Pull on both the short and long ends to tighten the knot on the needle, keeping the tension of both strands even.

How to Cast On

Before you knit you must get stitches onto the needle. You make your slip knot to begin, leaving a 6-inch (15cm) long tail, and then cast stitches onto your left needle for the required number of stitches. Although there are many ways to cast on, I have included three types of cast-ons: the Knit-on Cast-on and the Cable Cast-on, for beginning a project, and the Backwards Loop Cast-On, for adding stitches in the middle of a row.

1

2

3

Knit-On Cast-On

Once you have mastered the Knit-on method, you have actually learned the basic knit stitch, which is why this cast on is absolutely perfect for beginners.

1. Hold the needle with the slip knot in your left hand and the empty needle in your right hand. Hold the needles like a table knife. Insert the right needle from front to back under the left needle and through the stitch. With the yarn in your right hand, wrap the yarn around the right needle.

2. With the tip of the right needle, pull the yarn that you wrapped back through the stitch on the left needle and bring it to the front. Voila! One stitch is made!

3. Slip the new stitch back onto the left needle. Repeat steps 1 to 3 until you have the required number of stitches. (For a more advanced method that is perfect for ribbing, continue on to step 4.)

Cable Cast-On

The cable cast-on is a variation of the knit-on cast-on, and is used to form a sturdy, yet elastic edge that is excellent for ribbing.

4

4. Work as for the Knit-on Cast-on, except insert the needle between the stitches rather than into a stitch.

Backwards Loop Cast-On

When you need to add stitches in the middle of a row (to create a buttonhole, for example) you use this method to cast on.

1. Hold the needle with the slip knot in your right hand. Wrap the yarn around your left thumb so the yarn coming from the ball is in front of the loop.

2. Slip the needle under the loop and tighten the loop, as shown. Repeat for as many stitches as you need.

HOLDING NEEDLES AND YARN

There are many ways to hold the needles but the two most common are the knife hold (hands above the needles), and the pencil hold (hands below the needles). I think the knife hold gives you more control. Some knitters wrap the yarn around the index finger, but I don't do any complicated wrapping of the yarn. I think you can control your tension more easily without wrapping.

The most common style of knitting in English-speaking countries—and the method I am teaching you—is known as the English or American style. You hold the working yarn and control the tension of the yarn with your right hand, and the resulting fabric is smooth and strong. Another style is the Continental style, where you hold and control you yarn in your left hand. You may eventually want to learn both styles, but starting with the English or American style is the best way to begin.

Jil's Tip

Working at a table makes it easier to manage your work as you are learning to knit.

The Basic Knit Stitch

The knit stitch is the first stitch you will learn, and by doing the Knit-on Cast-on, you already know the basics. The first row is always the trickiest because you're working so close to the needle and the tension hasn't been fully established. But after knitting a few rows you'll be on your way.

1

2

1. Hold the needle with the cast-on stitches in your left hand and the empty needle in your right hand. Insert the right needle from front to back into the first stitch on the left needle and wrap the yarn just like in the first step of the cast-on.

2. With the tip of your right needle, pull the wrap through the stitch on the left needle and onto the right needle. Remove the stitch from the left needle so the new stitch is on the right needle. Repeat steps 1 and 2 until you have knit all the stitches from the left needle onto the right needle. Turn the work and hold the needle with the new stitches in the left hand and continue knitting back and forth. You'll be surprised how easy it is!

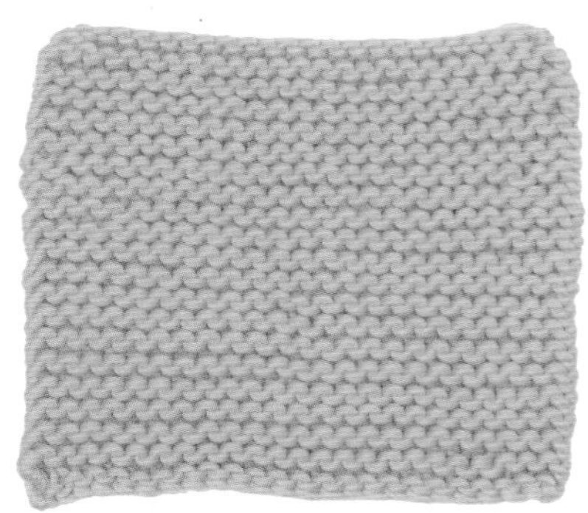

The garter stitch

The Garter Stitch

The garter stitch is the most basic form of knitting, essential to learning to knit. When working on straight needles, you knit every row. When working on a circular needle, or knitting in the round, you knit one row, and then purl one row. Garter stitch uses quite a bit more yarn than other stitches, is completely reversible, and makes a fabric that is thick and warm.

LESSON 2

How to Bind Off

When you are ready to finish your knitting, you have to bind off, sometimes called cast off, so the stitches do not unravel. As with casting on, there are several ways to bind off. I will begin with the easiest method and introduce you to a few other bind-offs later in the book.

> **Jil's Tip**
> To avoid a bound off edge that is too tight, bind off with a needle one size larger.

1. Hold the needle with the knitting in your left hand and the empty needle in your right hand. Knit the first two stitches. With the left needle in front of the right needle, insert the tip of the left needle into the first stitch on the right needle and pull it over the second stitch and off the right needle, as shown. You have bound off one stitch.

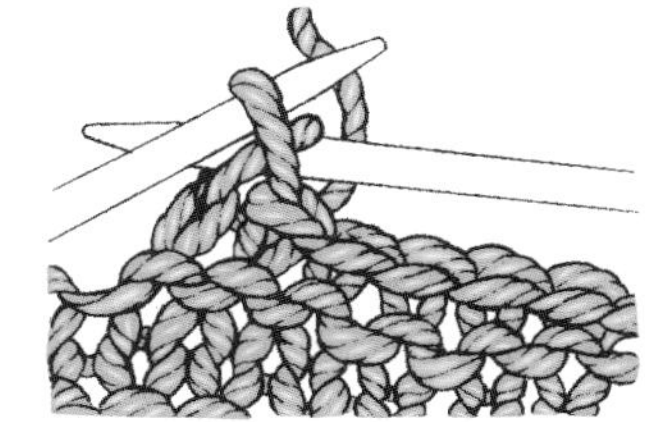

2. Knit the next stitch, pull the first over the second again and off the needle. Repeat across the row until all the stitches are bound off. Cut your yarn, leaving at least a 6-inch (15cm) tail. Slip the last stitch off the needle, bring the tail through the loop, and pull to close the loop.

How to Weave In Ends

Always leave at least a 6-inch (15cm) tail when casting on or joining another yarn ball.

> **Jil's Tip**
> I weave the ends in after I finish each section of my garment, which makes the final finishing easier and creates a neater project overall.

1. With the yarn tail threaded into a tapestry needle, and working on the wrong side of the fabric, weave the yarn under the loops on the back of the stitches, going three stitches up, three down, then three up again.

2. Snip off the excess yarn.

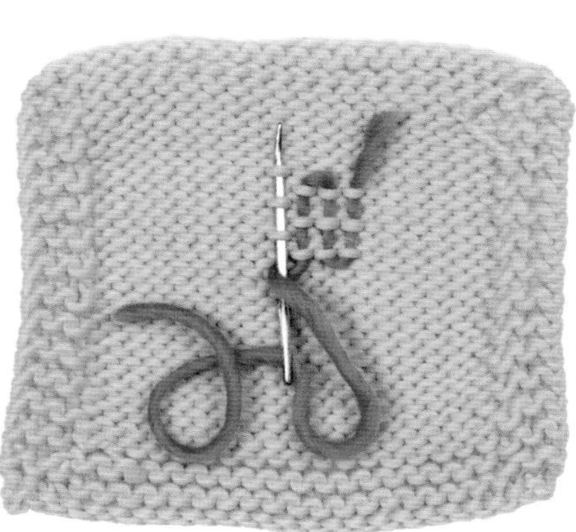

How to Make Pompoms

I always make my pompoms, big or small, much fuller than usually done, to make a stylish adornment for any garment.

1

1. Wrap yarn around four fingers fifty times. Remove your fingers and wrap an 18-inch (45.5-cm) strand of yarn twice around the center. Pull snug and tie twice.

2

2. Cut the loops on both sides.

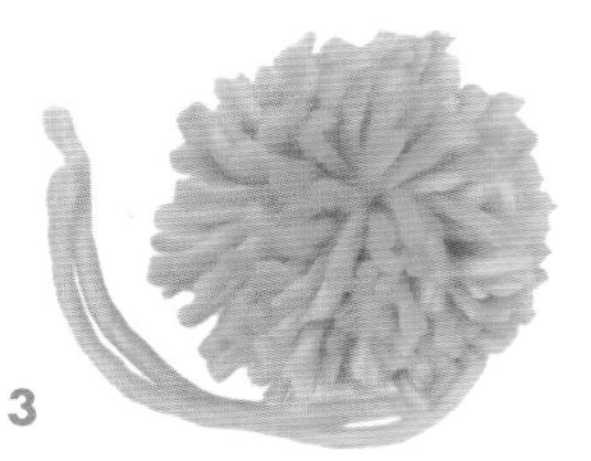

3

3. Trim the ends to form a pompom. Use the 18-inch (45.5-cm) strand to attach to the garment.

THE BALL BAND

The label that wraps around a ball of yarn contains a lot of important information: the fiber content and in what percentages, the weight and length, and the needle size. Remember that the needle size stated for the gauge on the ball band is only a recommendation; always do your gauge swatch! And do your swatch using the needles you will be using; different needles can give you a different gauge on the same yarn.

PROJECT:

learn-to-knit scarf with pompoms

Sample in photograph knit in Jil Eaton MinnowMerino (50g/77yds): #4755 Cerise (MC); Classic Elite Yarns La Gran Mohair (42g/90yds): #61532 Positively Pink (CC). Knit by Jil Eaton.

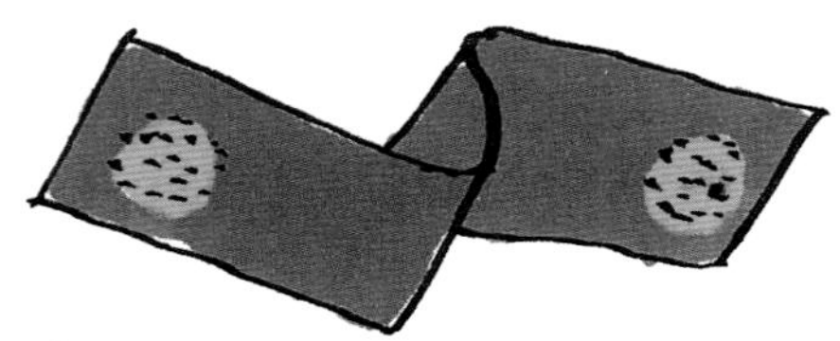

PROJECT:

learn-to-knit scarf with pompoms

A perky garter-stitch scarf adorned with two giant mohair pompoms is a great project for your first knitting foray. The scarf works up quickly, and the pompoms provide a bit of flair. A cozy antidote to the chill winter air, the scarf would make the perfect present.

Skills

cast on .... page **30**
knit stitch .... page **32**
bind off .... page **33**
pompoms .... page **34**

Finished Size

5½" (14cm) wide by 42" (106.5cm) long

Materials

- 230 yards (215m) worsted weight yarn (4) in MC
- 20 yards (18m) mohair yarn (4) in CC
- One pair size 8 (5mm) needles, *or size needed to obtain gauge*
- Tapestry needle

Gauge

18 stitches and 36 rows = 4" (10cm) in garter stitch

Scarf

With MC, cast on 25 stitches. Work in garter stitch (knit every row) for 42" (106.5cm). Bind off stitches loosely.

Finishing

With tapestry needle, weave in ends.

Make two 3-inch pompoms with CC and attach them 2¾" (7cm) from each end and centered on the scarf.

Jil's Tip
Always read the pattern all the way through before beginning!

LESSON 3

How to Make the Simplest Decrease

To decrease means to reduce the number of stitches. There are several ways to do that but the simplest is knit two together.

> **Jil's Tip**
> Knit two stitches together through the back of the stitches for a right slant, and through the front of the stitches for a left slant finish.

Knit Two Together (K2tog)

This stitch is the one used most often to decrease.

1. Hold the needle with the knitted fabric in your left hand and hold the empty needle in your right hand. Insert the right needle from front to back through the first two stitches knitwise, going from the left to right through both stitches on the left needle.

2. Wrap the yarn and pull through the two stitches as you would if you were knitting one, as shown. Drop the two stitches from the left needle. One new stitch is made from two stitches, and you have decreased one stitch.

2

How to Sew a Simple Seam

There are many ways to sew seams, but the basic running stitch is the simplest. Thread a tapestry needle with the same yarn as your project. After you have completed your knitting and blocked the pieces, place them with right sides together.

1. Using T-pins, pin the seam lining up the edges of both pieces.

2. Place your needle just under the edge stitch, and go down behind a few stitches and come back up in the front. Repeat across.

3. Keep your stitches small and even, and keep your tension the same as your knitting tension. Pulling too tight will cause the seam to pucker.

2

KNITWISE AND PURLWISE

When directions say to insert the needle knitwise, it means to go from left to right as you would if you were knitting the stitch. Purlwise means to insert the needle from right to left as you do when you purl (see page 46).

> **Jil's Tip**
> Sew seams with the same tension as your knitting.

PROJECT:

zany puppetina

How adorable is this frisky critter, complete with a shaggy mane and fiery tongue? A toy is fun to knit and even more fun to play with, and is a good way to use up leftover yarn. The puppet makes a charming present for both the young and the young at heart.

Skills

knit stitch .... page **32**
decrease .... page **37**
sewing a seam .... page **37**

Finished Size

10" (25.5cm) long

Materials

- 65 yards (60 m) worsted weight yarn (4) in MC and 2 yards (1.8 meters) each in A, B, C, and D
- One pair size 8 (5mm) needles, *or size needed to obtain gauge*
- Tapestry needle
- 2 buttons, ¾" (19mm) wide

Gauge

18 stitches and 36 rows = 4" (10cm) in garter stitch

Puppet

With MC, cast on 38 stitches.

Rows 1–8 Knit.

Row 9 K2tog, knit to last two stitches, k2tog.

Repeat the last 9 rows 7 times more—22 stitches.

Rows 10 and 11 Knit.

Row 12 K2tog, knit to last two stitches, k2tog.

Repeat the last three rows once more—18 stitches.

Next row K2tog across—9 stitches. Cut yarn, leaving a long tail, and thread through remaining stitches.

Finishing

Tongue

Cut six 12" (30.5cm) strands of A. Tie a knot near one end and make a braid using double strands. Tie another knot near the end of the braid.

Mane

Wrap one strand each of B, C and D around four fingers twenty times. Cut loops at one end and sew opposite end into seam of puppet as follows: With RS facing, pull long tail of MC snug and sew back seam while securing tongue at front of puppet, and mane between 2" (5cm) from front and 4" (10cm) from back of puppet.

Eyes

Sew on button eyes 1" (2.5cm) from front of puppet and ½" (1.25cm) down from seam.

Jil's Tip

Make sure to take breaks from your knitting to stretch your body and your hands.

Sample in photograph knit in Jil Eaton MinnowMerino (50g/77yds): #4794 Jade (MC), #4758 Rouge (A), #4789 Pinque (B), #4788 Tangerine (C) and #4755 Cerise (D). Buttons by Zecca. Knit by Jil Eaton.

LESSON 4

How to Join a New Yarn

You will have to join a new ball of yarn when you run out of yarn or when you change colors.

1. Leaving a 6-inch (15cm) tail of the original yarn, begin knitting with the new color leaving another 6-inch (15cm) tail.

2. You can weave in the two ends later. I prefer weaving in ends as I complete each part of the project, keeping my knitting neat and manageable.

How to Make a Three-Needle Bind-Off

This technique, called a knitted-seam bind-off, makes a beautiful even seam as you bind off two pieces together. Worked on the right side of the garment, this gives a design detail and definition to a shoulder. For the seam on the outside, hold these two pieces with the wrong sides facing each other. If you want the seam on the inside of the garment, hold the pieces with right sides together.

1. Hold two pieces of knitting with the needles parallel in your left hand. With a third needle knit through the first stitch on both needles, as shown, and move it to the right needle.

2. Knit through the second stitch on both needles, and pass the first stitch over the second. Continue in this way across until all your stitches are bound off.

A three-needle bind-off

RIGHT FROM WRONG

It's important to identify the right and wrong sides of your knitting because certain techniques are done only on the right side. In the garter stitch, both sides look the same; to make sure you have the right side attach a split-ring marker on the right side after knitting a few rows. On the stockinette stitch, the right side has a smooth appearance, rows of Vs, and the wrong side has the bumps. You can place a marker on the right side if you wish.

How to Pick Up Stitches

When you are adding a border to your garment, such as a neckband, or if you are knitting a sleeve from the top down, you will need to pick up stitches along a finished edge, which is called "pick up and knit." Use a needle one or two sizes smaller than the needles you are using to knit, changing back to the original size needle on the first knit row. Always work on the right side. If you are going to change the color of the added piece, pick up with the main color, and add the new color on the first knit row.

> **Jil's Tip**
> To pick up stitches evenly along an edge, place T-pins evenly along the edge and calculate how many stitches you need between markers.

1. Insert the needle between the edge stitch and the next stitch and catch a loop from the new ball of yarn around the needle tip. Pull up the loop, as shown.

2. Continue this way until you have picked up the required number of stitches.

1

How to Make a Single Crochet Edging

A simple single crochet stitch is the perfect way to finish the edge of a garment. It is often used around necklines for a smooth look.

1. Using a crochet hook the same size as your needles, place your crochet hook into the edge of the knit fabric and pull up a loop of yarn.

2. Yarn over the hook and pull through both loops on the hook. Repeat in each stitch across.

A single crochet edging

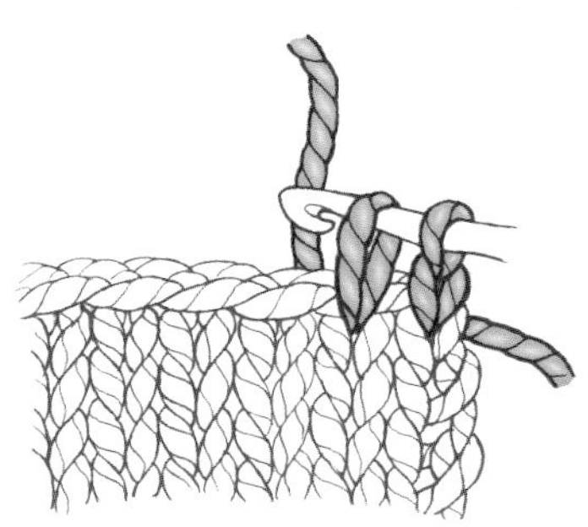

1

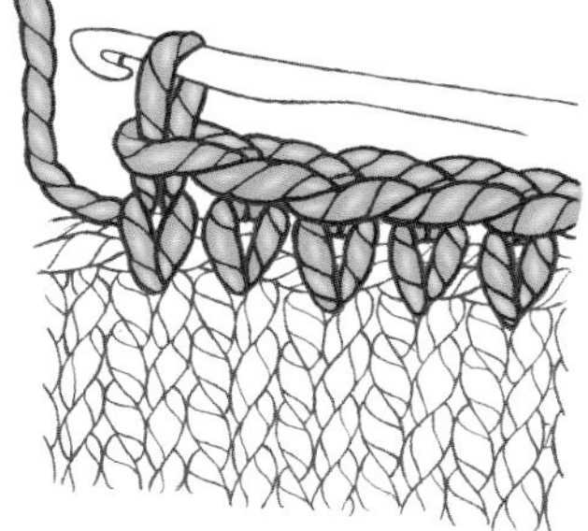

2

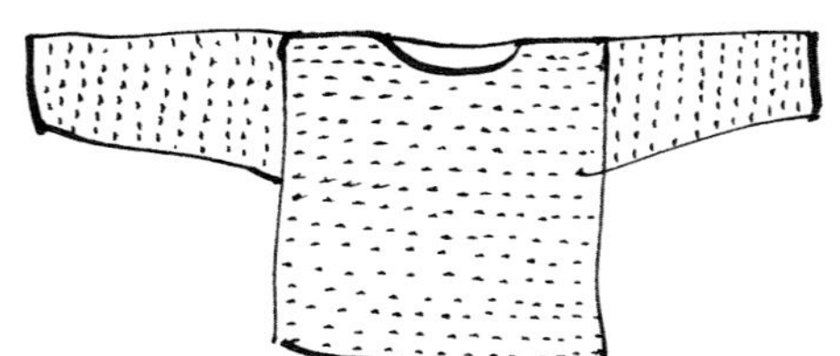

PROJECT:

crew sweater

This garter stitch pullover is a true classic and it is sized for unisex knitters from extra-small to extra-large. Easy to knit, and warm to wear, this sweater is sure to become a staple in your wardrobe.

Skills

knit stitch .... page **32**
joining a new yarn .... page **40**
picking up stitches .... page **41**
three-needle bind-off .... page **40**
sewing a seam .... page **37**
single crochet edging .... page **41**

Sizes

- XS (S, M, L, XL)
- Finished bust 36 (40, 44, 48, 52)" (91.5 [101.5, 111.5, 122, 132]cm)
- Finished length 24 (25, 26, 27, 28)" (61 [63.5, 66, 68.5, 71]cm)

Materials

- 1270 (1440, 1610, 1750, 1935) yards (1165 [1320, 1475, 1600, 1770]m) worsted-weight yarn (4)
- One pair size 8 (5mm) needles, *or size needed to obtain gauge*
- 3 size 8 (5mm) double-pointed needles
- 4 stitch holders
- 4 stitch markers
- One size H-8 (5mm) crochet hook
- Tapestry needle

Gauge

18 stitches and 32 rows = 4" (10cm) in garter stitch, stretched slightly vertically

Back

With straight needles, cast on 81 (90, 99, 108, 117) stitches. Work in garter stitch (knit every row) for 24 (25, 26, 27, 28)" (61 [63.5, 66, 68.5, 71]cm), end after working a wrong-side row.

Shape Shoulders and Neck

Next row (RS) K 25 (28, 31, 35, 39) and place these stitches on holder for right shoulder, bind off next 31 (34, 37, 38, 39) stitches for back neck, knit to end and place remaining 25 (28, 31, 35, 39) stitches on another holder for left shoulder.

Jil's Tip

Use removable markers to keep track when casting on a large number of stitches, placing a marker every twenty or twenty-five stitches.

Sample in photograph knit in Jil Eaton MinnowMerino (50g/77yds): #4716 Lamb's White. Knit by Peesh McCallahan and Mark Dube.

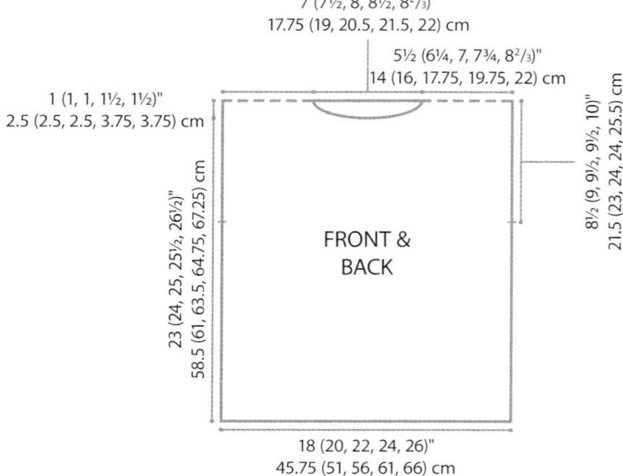

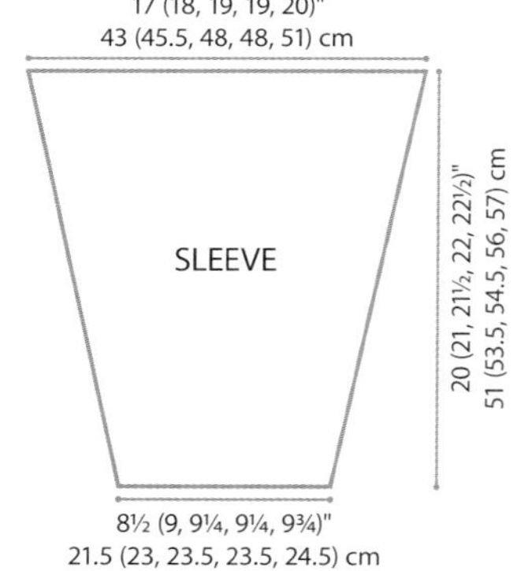

Jil's Tip
If you are a beginner, it is much easier to knit with lighter colors.

Front

Work as Back until piece measures 23 (24, 25, 25½, 26½)" (58.5 [61, 63.5, 64.75, 67.25]cm) from the beginning, end after working a wrong-side row.

Shape Right Neck and Shoulder

Next row (RS) K 33 (37, 41, 45, 49), place remaining 48 (53, 58, 63, 68) stitches on holder. Turn.

Next row (WS) Bind off 4 (4, 5, 5, 5) stitches, knit to end—29 (33, 36, 40, 44) stitches.

Knit one row.

Next row (WS) Bind off 2 (3, 3, 3, 3) stitches, knit to end—27 (30, 33, 37, 41) stitches.

Next row (RS) Knit to last two stitches, k2tog.

Knit one row.

Repeat the last two rows once more—25 (28, 31, 35, 39) stitches.

Work even, if necessary, until Front measures same length as Back to shoulder, end after working a wrong-side row. Place stitches on holder.

Shape Left Neck and Shoulder

With right side facing, place stitches on holder back to left needle, ready for a right-side row.

Next row (RS) Join yarn and bind off center 15 (16, 17, 18, 19) stitches, knit to end—33 (37, 41, 45, 49) stitches.

Knit one row.

Next row (RS) Bind off 4 (4, 5, 5, 5) stitches, knit to end—29 (33, 36, 40, 44) stitches.

Knit one row.

Next row (RS) Bind off 2 (3, 3, 3, 3) stitches, knit to end—27 (30, 33, 37, 41) stitches.

Knit one row.

Next row (RS) K2tog, knit to end.

Knit one row.

Repeat the last two rows once more—25 (28, 31, 35, 39) stitches.

Work even, if necessary, until Front measures same length as Back to shoulder, end after working a wrong-side row. Place stitches on holder.

Shoulder Seams

With right sides facing each other, and front of sweater facing you, place stitches of back and front left shoulders on two parallel double-pointed needles. The seam will be visible on wrong side of sweater. Work a three-needle bind-off as follows: With a third double-pointed needle, knit first stitch from front needle together with first stitch from back needle, *knit next stitch from front and back needles together, slip first stitch over the second stitch to bind off; repeat from * until all stitches are bound off. Cut yarn and pull end through loop. Repeat for right shoulder.

Sleeves

For armholes, place markers 8½ (9, 9½, 9½, 10)" (21.5 [23, 24, 24, 25.5]cm) down from shoulder seams on Front and Back.

With right side facing and straight needles, pick up and knit 77 (81, 86, 86, 90) stitches evenly spaced between markers.

Knit six rows.

Decrease row (RS) K2tog, knit to last two stitches, k2tog.

Knit seven rows.

Decrease row (RS) K2tog, knit to last 2 sts, k2tog.

Repeat last eight rows 16 (9, 15, 17, 16) times more.

Knit five rows.

Decrease row (RS) K2tog, knit to last two stitches, k2tog.

Repeat last six rows 0 (8, 4, 2, 4) times more—39 (41, 42, 42, 44) stitches.

Work even in garter stitch until piece measures 20 (21, 21½, 22, 22½)" (51 [53.5, 54.5, 56, 57]cm).

Bind off stitches loosely.

Finishing

Sew side and sleeve seams.

Neck Edging

Beginning at left shoulder seam, work one row of single crochet around the neck edge. Cut the yarn and pull through last single crochet loop to finish.

Weave in ends.

LESSON 5

The Basic Purl Stitch

The purl stitch is essentially the opposite of the knit stitch. Instead of pulling the wrapped yarn towards you, you will push it through the back of the stitch. Because it is more difficult to see what you are doing, the purl stitch is a bit harder to learn than the knit stitch, but with practice it becomes just as easy. The knit stitch and the purl stitch are the basics of knitting. When you knit one row, then purl one row, you create the stockinette stitch.

1. Hold the needle with the cast-on stitches in your left hand, and hold the empty needle in your right hand. Insert the right needle from back to front, into the first stitch on the left needle, and wrap the yarn counterclockwise around the needle, as shown.

2. With the tip of the right needle, pull the wrap through the stitch on the left needle and onto the right needle, as in the knit stitch. Drop the stitch from the left needle. A new stitch is made on the right needle. Continue in this way across the row.

The Stockinette Stitch

The stockinette stitch is the most common knitting stitch, made with knit and purl stitches, the basis of all knitting. On straight needles you knit on the right side, and purl on the wrong side. On a circular needle, you simply knit every row.

Reverse stockinette stitch is simply the stockinette stitch with the purl side on the front. To make it on straight needles you purl on the right side, and knit on the wrong side. On a circular needle, you simply purl every row.

The stockinette stitch

How to Make an Invisible Seam

The invisible seam, called mattress stitch, is a fabulous way to seam your garments. When done correctly you cannot see the seam. Always work this seam with the right sides of the work facing you, and join the edges row by row.

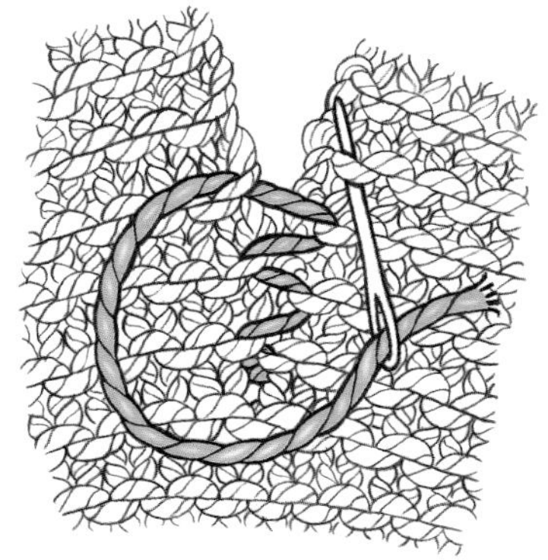

1. Lay the two pieces side by side on your worktable with the right sides facing you. You will be working from side to side connecting the bumps at the edge. Working from the bottom up, insert the yarn needle into the bottom loop on one side, then into the bottom loop of the corresponding stitch on the other side.

2. Keep working this way until your seam is completed, pulling the yarn to bring the sides together as you work. Pull tight enough to bring the sides together, but not so tight that the seam has no flexibility. You want your seams to have the same tension as the rest of your knitting.

> **Jil's Tip**
> If you will be sewing a seam, leave a very long tail before casting on or after binding off and use it to stitch the seam.

TYPES OF SEAMS

Choose the type of seam that will give the most polished look to your project. Use a running stitch (page 37) for a firm seam, a three-needle bind-off (page 40) when you want a knitted bind-off, mattress stitch (above) when you want an invisible seam on vertical seams, and the kitchener stitch (page 108) when you want to graft two pieces together without a seam.

PROJECT:

easy-as-pie pullover

We all love a good basic pullover, and this one in worsted weight yarn is simple to knit and easy to wear. Switching colors in the same yarn is an easy way to customize your garment because the gauge stays the same. So don't be afraid to experiment with color here. Bring your own creativity to light by choosing a color that works for you.

Skills

knit stitch .... page **32**
purl stitch .... page **46**
picking up stitches .... page **41**
decrease .... page **37**
three-needle bind-off .... page **40**
invisible seam .... page **47**

Sizes

- XS (S, M, L, XL)
- Finished bust 34 (38, 42, 46, 50)" (86 [96.5, 106.5, 116.5, 127]cm)
- Finished length (with rolled edge) 19½ (20, 20½, 21, 21½)" (49.5 [51, 52, 53.5, 54.3]cm)

Materials

- 790 (875, 960, 1050, 1140) yards (775 [800, 880, 960, 1045]m) worsted-weight yarn (4)
- One pair size 8 (5mm) needles, *or size needed to obtain gauge*
- 3 size 8 (5mm) double-pointed needles
- 4 stitch holders
- 4 stitch markers
- Tapestry needle

Gauge

18 stitches and 24 rows = 4" (10cm) in stockinette stitch

Back

With straight needles, cast on 77 (86, 95, 104, 113) stitches. Work in stockinette stitch until piece measures 20 (20½, 21, 21½, 22)" (51 [52, 53.5, 54.5, 56]cm) from the beginning, end after working a wrong-side row.

Shape Shoulders and Neck

Next row (RS) K 24 (27, 31, 34, 38) and place these stitches on holder for right shoulder, bind off next 29 (32, 33, 36, 37) stitches for back neck, knit to end and place the remaining 24 (27, 31, 34, 38) stitches on another holder for left shoulder.

Sample in photograph knit in Jil Eaton MinnowMerino (50g/77yds): #4754 Lavender. Knit by Nita Young.

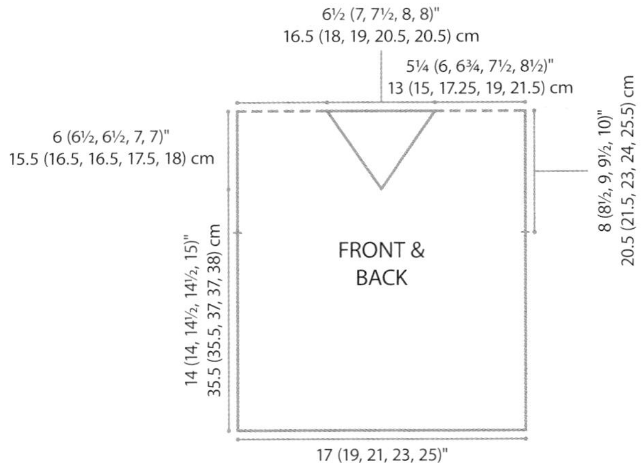

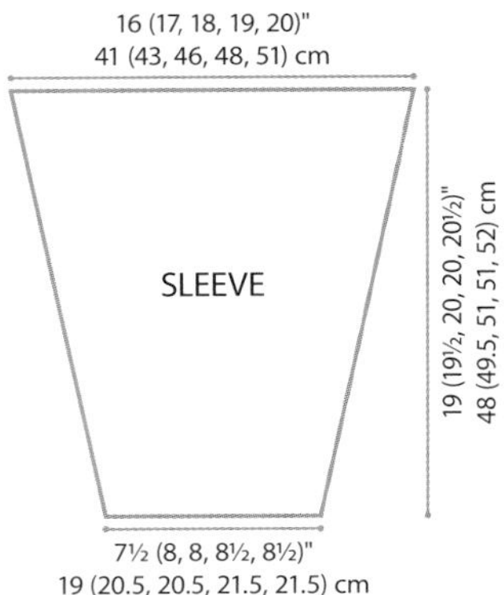

Front

Work as for Back until piece measures 14 (14, 14½, 14½, 15)" (35.5 [35.5, 37, 37, 38]cm) from the beginning, end after working a wrong-side row.

Shape Right Neck and Shoulder

Next row (RS) K 38 (43, 47, 52, 56), place remaining 39 (43, 48, 52, 57) stitches on holder. Turn.

Purl one row.

Next row (RS) Knit to last three stitches, k2tog, k1.

Repeat the last two rows 11 (13, 13, 16, 16) times more—26 (29, 33, 35, 39) stitches.

Work three rows.

Next row (RS) Knit to last three stitches, k2tog, k1.

Repeat the last four rows 1 (1, 1, 0, 0) times more—24 (27, 31, 34, 38) stitches.

Work even until Front measures the same length as Back to shoulder, end after working a wrong-side row. Place stitches on holder.

Shape Left Neck and Shoulder

With right side facing, return stitches on holder back to the left needle, ready for a right-side row.

Next row (RS) Join yarn and bind off center 1 (0, 1, 0, 1) stitch, knit to end—38 (43, 47, 52, 56) stitches.

Purl one row.

Next row (RS) K1, k2tog, knit to end.

Repeat the last two rows 11 (13, 13, 16, 16) times more—26 (29, 33, 35, 39) stitches.

Work three rows.

Next row (RS) K1, k2tog, knit to end.

Repeat the last four rows 1 (1, 1, 0, 0) times more—24 (27, 31, 34, 38) stitches.

Work even until Front measures same length as Back to shoulder, end after working a wrong-side row. Place stitches on holder.

Decrease row (RS) K2tog, knit to last two stitches, k2tog.

Repeat last six rows 14 (13, 9, 7, 4) times more.

Work three rows.

Decrease row (RS) K2tog, knit to last two stitches, k2tog.

Repeat last four rows 3 (5, 11, 14, 19) times more—34 (36, 36, 38, 38) stitches.

Work even until piece measures 19 (19½, 20, 20, 20½)" (48 [49.5, 51, 51, 52]cm). Bind off stitches.

Shoulder Seams

With wrong sides facing each other, and front of sweater facing you, place stitches of back and front left shoulders on two parallel double-pointed needles. The seam will be visible on right side of sweater. Work three-needle bind off (page 40). Cut yarn and pull end through loop. Repeat for right shoulder.

Sleeves

For armholes, place markers 8 (8½, 9, 9½, 10)" (20.5 [21.5, 23, 24, 25.5]cm) down from shoulder seams on Front and Back.

With right side facing and straight needles, pick up and knit 72 (76, 82, 86, 90) stitches evenly spaced between markers.

Beginning with a wrong-side row, work in stockinette stitch for five rows.

Decrease row (RS) K2tog, knit to last 2 sts, k2tog.

Work five rows.

Finishing

Work the side and sleeve seams as follows: sew seams from wrong side for ½" (1.25cm) from bottom and cuffs so that they are invisible at rolled edges, then push needle through and continue to work seams from right side.

LESSON 6

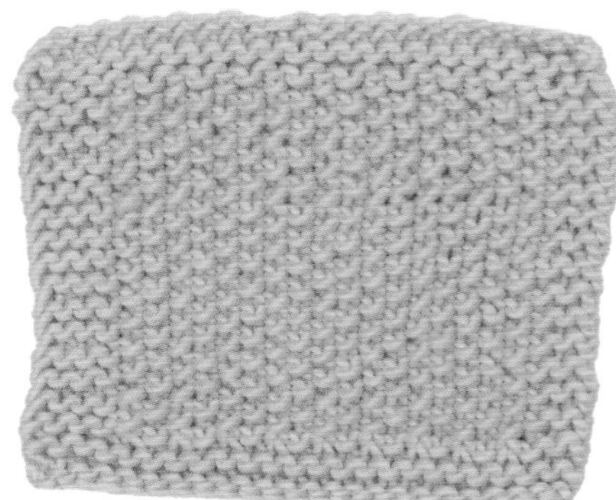
The seed stitch

The Seed Stitch

In contrast to the stockinette stitch, which is very smooth, the seed stitch has a textured pattern created by alternating knit and purl stitches. The seed stitch has charming definition, and creates a fabric that lays flat beautifully without any other finishing.

1. Knit 1, purl 1 across the row.
2. Continue on the next row, and all other rows, knitting all purl stitches and purling all knit stitches as they face you.

"AS THEY FACE YOU"

Sometimes pattern directions will say to work the stitches "as they face you" or "as they appear." This means to look at the stitch on the needle to see if it is a knit or a purl stitch. You can tell your stitches apart because they make different shapes: the knit stitch is smooth and forms a V, and the purl stitch has a little bump at the base. For seed stitch, you knit the purl stitches and purl the knit stitches.

PROJECT:
seedling pullover

Sample in photograph knit in Classic Elite Yarns Ariosa (50g/87yds): #4858 Lipstick. Knit by Donna Gross.

PROJECT:
seedling pullover

A pullover in seed stitch pattern with a crew neck is a wonderful compliment to your child's play clothes. The bulky weight provides extra warmth for chilly days, and the bright red color makes a bold fashion statement.

Skills

seed stitch .... page **52**
picking up stitches .... page **41**
three-needle bind-off.......... page **40**
sewing a seam.................... page **37**

Sizes

- 1 (2, 4, 6) years
- Finished chest 24 (26, 28, 30½)" (61 [66, 71, 77.5]cm)
- Finished length 11 (13, 15, 16)" (28 [33, 38, 40.5]cm)

Materials

- 315 (405, 530, 620) yards (290 [375, 490, 570]m) bulky weight yarn (5)
- One pair size 10½ (6.5mm) needles, *or size needed to obtain gauge*
- 3 size 10½ (6.5mm) double-pointed needles
- One size 10½ (6.5mm) circular needle, 16" (40.5cm) long
- 5 stitch holders
- 4 stitch markers
- Tapestry needle

Gauge

15 stitches and 28 rows = 4" (10cm) in seed stitch

Pattern Stitch

Seed Stitch (over an odd number of stitches)

Row 1 K1, *p1, k1; repeat from * to end.

Row 2 Knit the purl stitches, and purl the knit stitches, as they face you.

Repeat Row 2 for Seed Stitch.

Back

With straight needles, cast on 45 (49, 53, 57) stitches. Work in seed stitch until piece measures 11 (13, 15, 16)" (28 [33, 38, 40.5] cm from the beginning, end after working a wrong-side row.

Shape Shoulders and Neck

Next row (RS) Work 14 (15, 16, 17) and place these stitches on holder for right shoulder, work next 17 (19, 21 23) stitches and place these stitches on holder for back neck, work to end and place remaining 14 (15, 16, 17) stitches on another holder for left shoulder.

Front

Work as Back until piece measures 9½ (11½, 13½, 14½)" (24 [29, 34, 36.5]cm) from the beginning, end after working a wrong-side row.

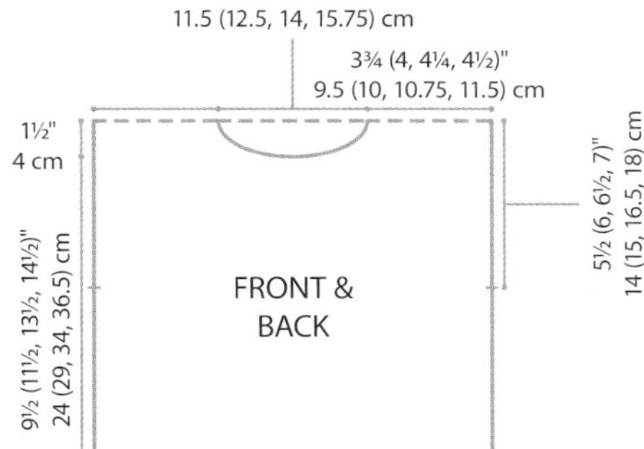

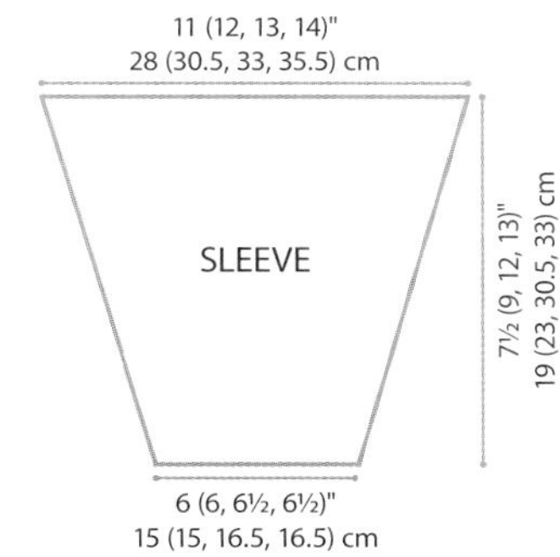

Shape Right Neck and Shoulder

Next row (RS) Work 18 (20, 21, 23), place remaining 27 (29, 32, 34) stitches on holder. Turn.

Next row (WS) Bind off three stitches, work to end—15 (17, 18, 20) stitches.

Next row (RS) Work to last two stitches, k2tog.

Work one row.

Repeat the last two rows 0 (1, 1, 2) times more—14 (15, 16, 17) stitches.

Work even until Front measures same length as Back to shoulder, end after working a wrong-side row. Place stitches on holder.

Shape Left Neck and Shoulder

With right side facing, return stitches on holder to left needle, ready for a right-side row.

Next row (RS) Join yarn and bind off center 9 (9, 11, 11) stitches, work to end—18 (20, 21, 23) stitches.

Work one row.

Next row (RS) Bind off three stitches, work to end—15 (17, 18, 20) stitches.

Work one row.

Next row (RS) K2tog, work to end.

Repeat the last two rows 0 (1, 1, 2) times more—14 (15, 16, 17) stitches.

Work even, if necessary, until Front measures same length as Back to shoulder, end after working a wrong-side row. Place stitches on holder.

Shoulder Seams

With wrong sides facing each other, and front of sweater facing you, place stitches of back and front left shoulders on two parallel double-pointed needles. Seam will be visible on right side of sweater. Work three-needle bind off (page 40). Cut yarn and pull end through loop. Repeat for right shoulder.

Sleeves

For armholes, place markers 5½ (6, 6½, 7)" (14 [15, 16.5, 18]cm) down from shoulder seams on Front and Back.

With right side facing and straight needles, pick up and knit 41 (45, 49, 53) stitches evenly spaced between markers. Continue in seed stitch beginning on Row 1.

Work for seven rows.

Decrease row (RS) K2tog, work to last two stitches, k2tog.

Repeat last eight rows 0 (0, 2, 0) times more.

Work for five rows.

Decrease row (RS) K2tog, work to last two stitches, k2tog.

Repeat last six rows 4 (5, 7, 11) times more.

Work for three rows.

Decrease row (RS) K2tog, work to last two stitches, k2tog.

Repeat last four rows 2 (3, 0, 0) times more—23 (23, 25, 25) stitches.

Work even until sleeve measures 7½ (9, 12, 13)" (19 [23, 30.5, 33]cm).

Bind off stitches loosely in seed stitch.

Finishing

Sew side and sleeve seams.
Weave in all loose ends.

Collar

With right side facing and circular needle, begin at left shoulder seam, pick up and knit 27 (27, 29, 29) stitches along front neck, knit 17 (19, 21, 23) stitches from back neck holder—44 (46, 50, 52) stitches. Join stitches, place marker for beginning of round, and work in rounds of seed stitch for 1½" (4cm). Bind off stitches loosely in seed stitch.

Jil's Tip
Row counting will make your garment pieces match perfectly.

LESSON 7

How to Increase

When you increase you are adding a number of stitches, sometimes evenly across a row and sometimes at the beginning or end of a row. The most common increase is to knit into both the front and the back of a stitch.

Knit One Front and Back (K1f&b)

Knit one front and back is just like knitting but doing it twice. It may seem a little awkward at first but with practice you'll get the hang of it.

1. Knit into the front of the stitch as usual, but do not remove it from the needle.

2. Pull your needle tip up and then knit into the back of the same stitch, as shown. Don't be afraid to pull some extra yarn in the first stitch so it is easy to make the second stitch.

3. Move both new stitches from the left needle to the right needle. This makes two stitches in one stitch.

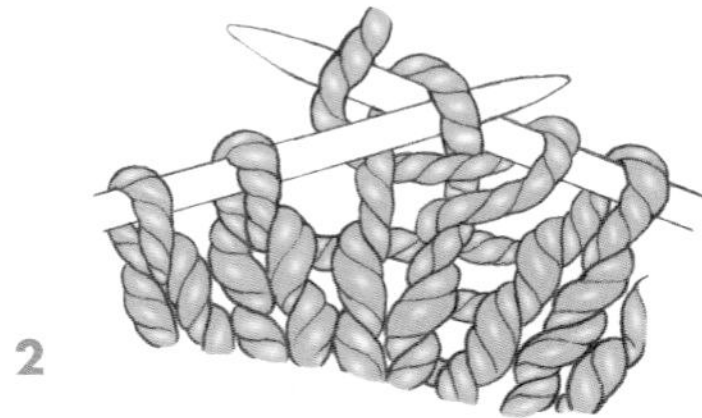

How to Felt

Felting happens when you wash knitted wool fabric in hot water in the washing machine. The change in water temperature and the agitation in the wash cycle make the fibers bind together and shrink, creating a wonderful, thick fabric. For best results wash in a top-loading machine with hot water and dish detergent. Different machines work differently, so try felting your swatch first to see how the fabric shrinks in your machine. Repeat the process if it doesn't felt down enough.

1. Set the washing machine on hot wash/cold rinse for a small load. Place the knitted item in the water with one teaspoon liquid dishwashing detergent.

2. Run the machine on the longest cycle, and then rinse with cold water. Check the item and repeat if necessary until the desired size is achieved. Remove the knitted item and let it air dry.

A knitted swatch before felting (top) and after felting (bottom)

PROJECT:

pooch jacket

Your beloved pup will be warm and dry in this weatherproof dog coat. Rain and snow roll right off, and a quick post-walk shake will keep it in good order, ready for the next outing.

Skills

knit stitch .... page **32**
purl stitch .... page **46**
increase .... page **57**
felting .... page **57**

Sizes

- Girth 18 (23, 28)" (45.5 [58.5, 71]cm)
- Finished length (neck to tail–before felting) 18½ (24½, 30)" (47 [62, 76]cm)
- Finished length (neck to tail–after felting) 13 (17, 21)" (33 [43, 53.5]cm)
- Finished width (at widest part–before felting) 21½ (30, 38½)" (54.5 [76, 97.5]cm)
- Finished width (at widest part–after felting) 15 (21, 27)" (38 [53.5, 68.5]cm)

Jil's Tip

Washable wool is meant to retain its shape in the wash so it will not felt. For projects to be felted, choose non-washable wool.

Materials

- 210 (345, 515) yards (195 [320, 475]m) heavy worsted weight 100% wool yarn (non-washable wool) (5)
- One pair size 10½ (6.5mm) needles, *or size needed to obtain gauge*
- 2 stitch markers
- Stitch holder
- 2" (5cm)-wide hook and loop tape, 9" (23cm)- long piece
- 3 buttons, 1½" (38mm) wide
- Tapestry needle

Gauge

13 stitches and 20 rows = 4" (10cm) in stockinette stitch before felting

18 stitches and 27 rows = 4" (10cm) in stockinette stitch after felting

Sample in photograph knit in Manos del Uruguay Clasica (100g/138yds): S Magenta. Buttons from Zecca. Knit by Shirley LaBranche.

Body

Beginning at the tail, cast on 30 (48, 66) stitches.

Next row (RS) K3, place marker, knit to last three stitches, place marker, k3.

Knit three rows.

Increase row 1 (RS) K3, increase one stitch in next stitch, knit to last four stitches, increase one stitch in next stitch, k3.

Increase row 2 K3, increase one stitch in next stitch, purl to last four stitches, increase one stitch in next stitch, k3.

Repeat the last two rows five times more—54 (72, 90) stitches.

Work even, keeping the first and last three stitches in garter stitch and the remaining stitches in stockinette stitch, until the piece measures 11½ (15¾, 20)" (29 [40, 51]cm) from the beginning, end after working a wrong-side row.

Shape Chest

Increase (RS) K3, increase one stitch in next stitch, knit to last four stitches, increase one stitch in next stitch, k3.

Work three rows.

Increase (RS) K3, increase one stitch in next stitch, knit to last four stitches, increase one stitch in next stitch, k3.

Repeat last four rows 2 (11, 14) times more—62 (98, 122) stitches.

For Small Size Only

Work five rows.

Increase (RS) K3, increase one stitch in next stitch, knit to last four stitches, increase one stitch in next stitch, k3.

Repeat last six rows twice more—68 stitches.

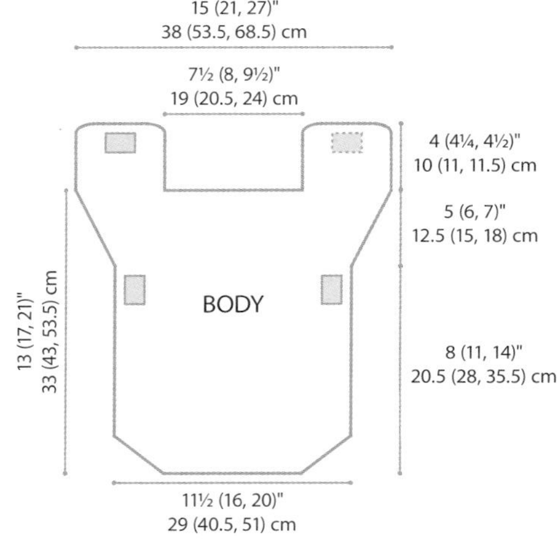

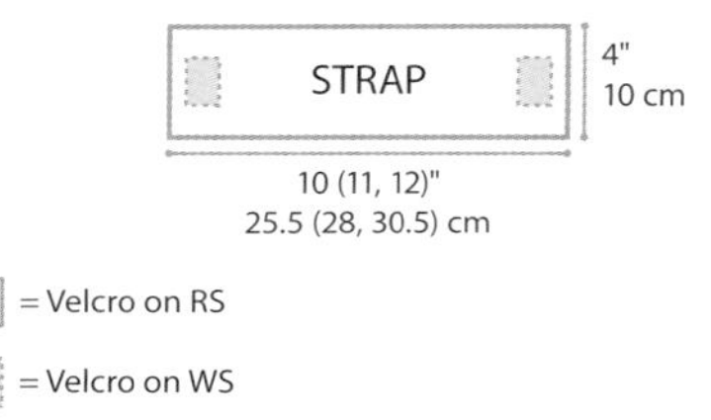

Diagram reflects measurements after felting.

For All Sizes

Work even on 68 (98, 122) stitches until piece measures 18 (24, 29½)" (45.5 [61, 75]cm) from the beginning, end after working a wrong-side row

Knit one row.

Next row (WS) K3, p 11 (24, 33), k 40 (44, 50), p 11 (24, 33), k3.

Repeat the last two rows once more.

Shape Right Neck Flap

Next row (RS) K 17 (30, 39), place remaining 51 (68, 83) stitches on holder.

*Keeping three stitches in garter stitch and remaining stitches in stockinette stitch, work even for 4¼ (4½, 5)" (11 [11.5, 12.5]cm), end after working a wrong-side row.

Decrease row **(RS)** K3, k2tog, knit to last five stitches, k2tog, k3.

Next row (WS) K3, purl to last three stitches, k3.

Repeat the last two rows twice more—11 (24, 33) stitches.

Knit four rows.

Bind off.*

Shape Left Neck Flap

With right side facing, place stitches on holder back to left needle, ready for a right-side row.

Next row (RS) Join yarn and bind off center 34 (38, 44) stitches, knit to end—17 (30, 39) stitches.

Repeat from * to * as for Right Neck Flap.

Strap

Cast on 18 stitches. Work in stockinette stitch until piece measures 14¼ (15¾, 17)" (36 [40, 43]cm) from the beginning.

Bind off stitches.

Felting

Felt the garment and strap (page 57). Due to temperature fluctuations, felting time will vary so check often for sizing. After checking the measurements, run through the cycle again if necessary. Remove the garment and strap, lay them flat, and let them air dry.

Finishing

Sew hook and loop tape to the wrong side of the strap and the right side of the garment, just behind chest shaping, or fit sweater on dog to determine placement of strap. Sew decorative buttons to the right side of the strap. Sew hook and loop tape to the right side of one neck flap and to the wrong side of the other neck flap. Sew one decorative button to the right side of the outer neck flap.

intermediate charmers

The projects in the chapter are designed specifically to hone your basic knitting skills and introduce new ones, too. Now that you are becoming more technically accomplished, try knitting stripes, creating buttonholes, and making cables. Whether you are knitting for yourself or a loved one, you'll enjoy these chic and charming patterns. Challenging yourself to learn new skills will greatly expand your knitting world.

PROJECT INDEX

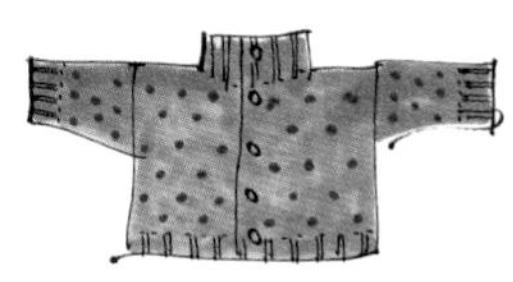

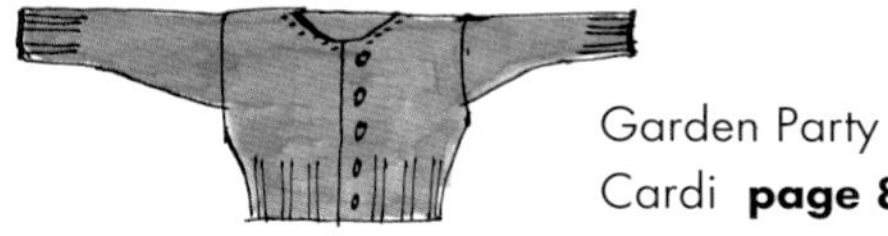

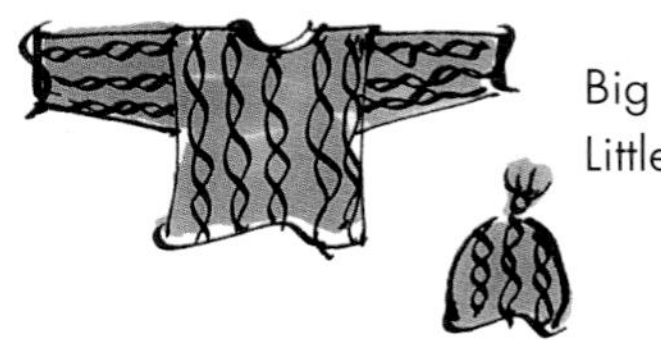

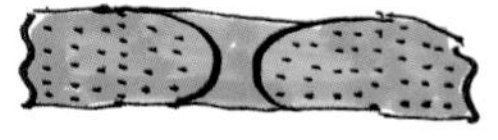

LESSON 8

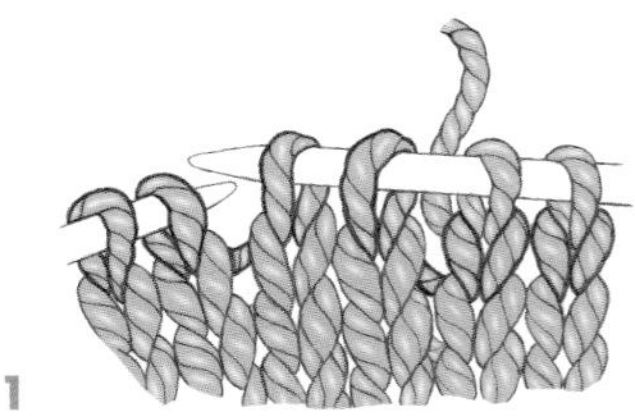
1

2

How to Make Another Decrease

When you decrease you are taking away a number of stitches to make your work smaller, sometimes evenly across a row and sometimes in one place only. See knit two together on page 37. Another one of the most common decreases is to slip, slip, knit.

Slip, Slip, Knit (ssk)

This decrease slants to the left and reduces two stitches to one.

1. On right side slip the next two stitches as if you were knitting.

2. Insert the tip of the left needle into the front of these two stitches at the same time, and knit them together as if they were one stitch.

Jil's Tip

On patterns that instruct you to increase or decrease at the beginning or end of a row, work the increases or decreases one or two stitches in from the edge to avoid steps at the edge.

How To Embroider

There are many ways to embroider on knit fabric, but these two, backstitch and French knot, use basic embroidery stitches that add charm to the knitting.

The Back Stitch

The back stitch creates a straight line and is good for outlining.

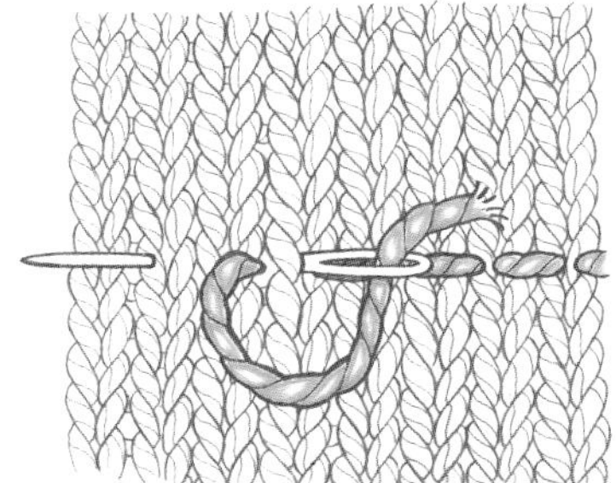

1. With a yarn or tapestry needle, and a length of a contrasting color yarn, bring the yarn to the front two stitches from the right edge, then go back two stitches to the right and go to the back of the fabric.

2. Bring the yarn back to the front two stitches to the left of the original insert point. Repeat these two steps.

The French Knot

The French knot is three-dimensional, perfect for creating eyes or other small features.

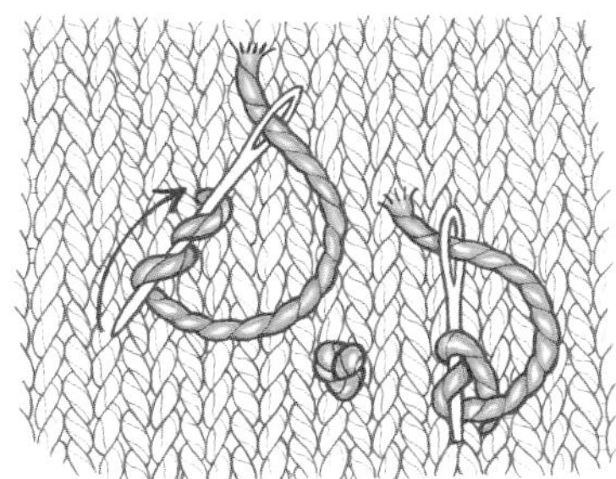

1. Bring the needle to the front, and wrap the yarn around the needle two or three times.

2. Hold the wraps down with your thumb, and pull the needle through the wraps. Pull the stitches tight and go back into the fabric near the place it came to the front, creating a three-dimensional knot on the right side of the fabric.

Jil's Tip

When picking up dropped stitches use a needle a few sizes smaller for an easier pick-up. I keep a small 16-inch circular needle in my kit for this purpose.

PROJECT:

duckie baby blanket

A cozy cotton bath blanket with corner hood and embroidered duck face makes bath time fun. The cotton yarn used is soft and absorbent, making this perfect for drying off and playing an after bath game of peek-a-boo. This project would make a wonderful baby shower present, too.

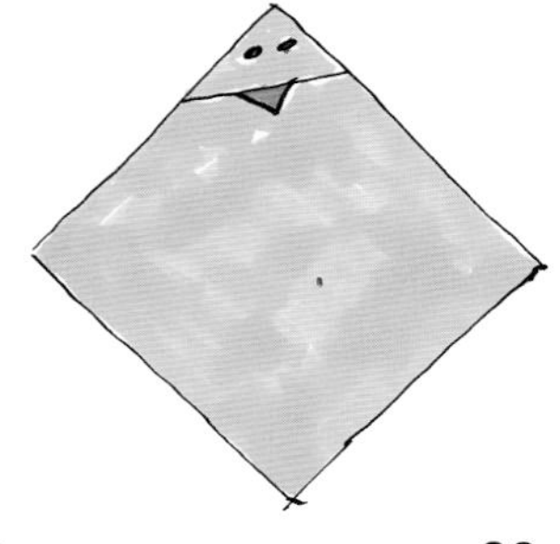

Skills

garter stitch .... page **32**
sewing a seam .... page **37**
embroidery .... page **65**

Finished size

30" (76cm) by 30" (76cm)

Materials

- 625 yards (575m) bulky weight cotton (5) in MC
- 5 yards (4.5m) worsted-weight yarn (4) in A and 1 yard (.9m) in B
- One size 9 (5.5mm) circular needle, 40" (101.5cm) long, *or size needed to obtain gauge*
- One pair size 8 (5mm) needles
- 2 stitch markers
- Tapestry needle

Gauge

15 stitches and 22 rows = 4" (10cm) in stockinette stitch using MC and larger needle

15 stitches and 32 rows = 4" (10cm) in garter stitch using MC and larger needle

Sample in photograph knit in Classic Elite Yarns Sprout (100g/109yds): #4350 Evening Primrose (MC); Jil Eaton MinnowMerino (50g/77yds): #4788 Tangerine (A) and #4793 Blue Bird (B). Knit by Pam Tessier.

Blanket

With circular needle and MC, cast on 113 stitches. Work back and forth in garter stitch (knit every row) for 3" (7.5cm), end after working a right-side row.

Next row (WS) K12, p89, k12.

Following RS row Knit.

Keeping the first and last twelve stitches in garter stitch and the center 89 stitches in stockinette stitch, work even until the piece measures 27" (68.5cm) from the beginning. Continue in garter stitch over all stitches for 3" (7.5cm) more. Bind off stitches.

Hood

With circular needle and MC, cast on 58 stitches.

Next row Knit.

Decrease row (RS) K1, k2tog, knit to last three stitches, slip two stitches and knit together, k1.

Repeat the last two rows 27 times more—2 stitches. Bind off stitches.

Jil's Tip

Natural yarns such as wool and cotton are best for knitting for babies.

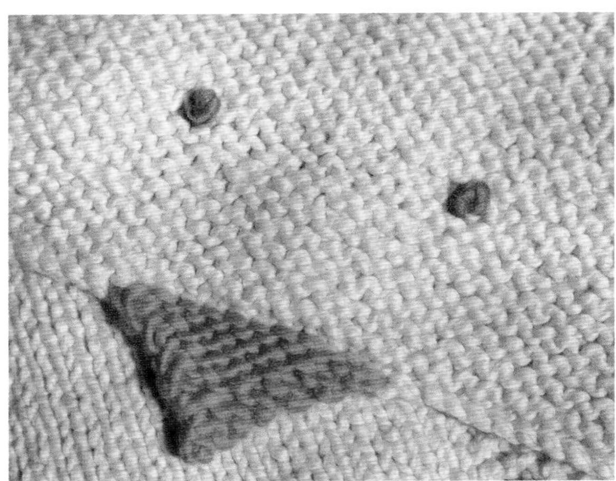

Finishing

Beak

Place markers 1½" (4cm) to the left and right of the center of the cast-on edge of the hood. With straight needles and A, and right side facing, pick up and knit thirteen stitches between markers.

Next row Knit.

Decrease row (RS) K1, k2tog, knit to last three stitches, slip two stitches and knit together, k1.

Repeat the last two rows five times more—1 stitch. Cut yarn and pull through last stitch.

Eyes

With a double strand of B and tapestry needle, make two French knots at the corners of the beak, 2½" (6.5cm) up from the cast-on edge of the hood.

Sew the side edges of the hood to any corner of the blanket.

LESSON 9

How to Make Stripes

Making stripes is the easiest way to introduce color into your work. If the stripes are relatively small you can carry your second color up the side of the piece. If the stripes are more than one inch (2.5cm) wide, you will have to snip the ends, leaving 6-inch (15cm) tails for weaving in later.

1. With color A work in pattern stitch for two rows.
2. Join color B and work two rows, carrying color A up the side, as shown.
3. Work two rows A, and repeat Steps 2 and 3.

NO KNOTS

If you come to a knot in your yarn, cut it, leaving a six-inch (15cm) tail, and begin again, after leaving another six-inch (15cm) tail. Don't try to put the knot to the back and continue knitting because knots can come undone or poke through to the front of the work.

Striped pattern made by working two rows of each color

PROJECT:

striped tee

Saucy and bright, this striped tee shirt is perfect for warm weather wear. Dress it down with crisp jeans, or dress it up with a short summer skirt. Cotton is the best fiber for summer knitting projects—it's cool to knit with and comfortable to wear.

Skills

stockinette stitch .... page **46**
decrease .... page **37**
increase.............................. page **37**
sewing a seam.................. page **57**
single crochet edging......... page **41**

Sizes

- S (M, L)
- Finished bust 36 (40, 44)" (91.5 [101.5, 111.5]cm)
- Finished length 20 (21½, 23)" (51 [54.5, 58.5]cm)

Materials

- 360 (440, 520) yards (330 [405, 480]m) worsted-weight cotton yarn (4)
- One pair size 8 (5mm) needles, *or size needed to obtain gauge*
- 3 Size 8 (5mm) double-pointed needles
- One size 6 (4mm) circular needle, 16" (40.5cm) long
- 4 stitch holders
- 4 stitch markers
- One size H-8 (5mm) crochet hook
- Tapestry needle

Gauge

17 stitches and 24 rows = 4" (10cm) in stockinette stitch and stripe pattern

Stitch Pattern

Stripe Pattern

Row 1 (RS) Knit with MC.

Row 2 Purl with MC.

Row 3 Knit with CC.

Row 4 Purl with CC.

Repeat Rows 1–4 for Stripe Pattern.

Sample in photograph knit in Knit One Crochet Too Cotonade (50g/83yds): #372 Melon (MC) and #337 Cantaloupe (CC). Knit by Lucinda Heller.

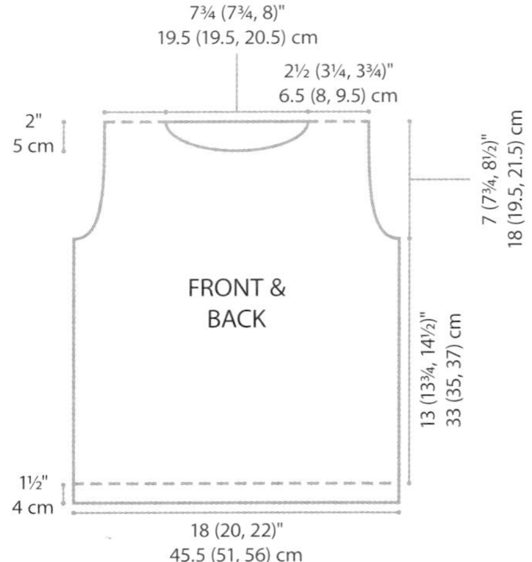

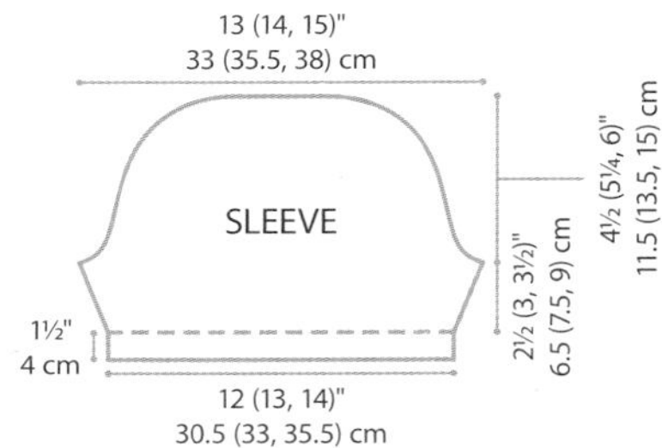

Back

With straight needles and MC, cast on 77 (85, 94) stitches. Work in stockinette stitch for seven rows.

Next row (WS) Knit for turning ridge.

Continue in stripe pattern until piece measures 13 (13¾, 14½)" (33 [35, 37]cm) from turning ridge.

Shape Armholes

Bind off 3 (4, 4) stitches at the beginning of the next four rows—65 (69, 78) stitches

Decrease row (RS) K2tog, knit to last two stitches, k2tog.

Purl one row.

Repeat the last two rows 4 (3, 5) times more—55 (61, 66) stitches.

Work even until armholes measure 7 (7¾, 8½)" (18 [19.5, 21.5]cm), end after working a wrong-side row.

Shape Shoulders and Neck

Next row (RS) K 11 (14, 16) and place these stitches on holder for right shoulder, bind off next 33 (33, 34) stitches for back neck, knit to end and place remaining 11 (14, 16) stitches on another holder for left shoulder.

Front

Work as Back until armholes measure 5 (5¾, 6½)" (12.5 [14.5, 16.5]cm), end after working a wrong-side row.

Shape Right Neck and Shoulder

Next row (RS) K 20 (23, 25), place remaining 57 (62, 69) stitches on holder. Turn.

Next row (WS) Bind off four stitches, purl to end—16 (19, 21) stitches.

Knit one row.

Next row (WS) Bind off two stitches, purl to end—14 (17, 19) stitches.

Next row (RS) Knit to last two stitches, k2tog.

Purl one row.

Repeat the last two rows twice more—11 (14, 16) stitches.

Work even until Front measures same length as Back to shoulder, end after working a wrong-side row. Place stitches on holder.

Shape Left Neck and Shoulder

With right side facing, place stitches on holder back to left needle, ready for a right-side row.

Next row (RS) Join color in progress and bind off center 15 (15, 16) stitches, knit to end—20 (23, 25) stitches.

Purl one row.

Next row (RS) Bind off 4 stitches, knit to end—16 (19, 21) stitches.

Purl one row.

Next row (RS) Bind off two stitches, knit to end—14 (17, 19) stitches.

Purl one row.

Next row (RS) K2tog, knit to end.

Purl one row.

Repeat the last two rows twice more—11 (14, 16) stitches.

Work even until Front measures same length as Back to shoulder, end after working a wrong-side row. Place stitches on holder.

Sleeves

With straight needles and MC, cast on 51 (55, 60) stitches. Work in stockinette stitch for seven rows.

Next row (WS) Knit for turning ridge.

Continue in stripe pattern for eight rows.

Increase row (RS) Increase in first stitch, knit to last stitch, increase in last stitch.

Work 5 (7, 7) rows

Increase row (RS) Increase in first stitch, knit to last stitch, increase in last stitch—55 (59, 64) stitches.

Work even until piece measures 2½ (3, 3½)" (6.5 [7.5, 9]cm) from turning ridge.

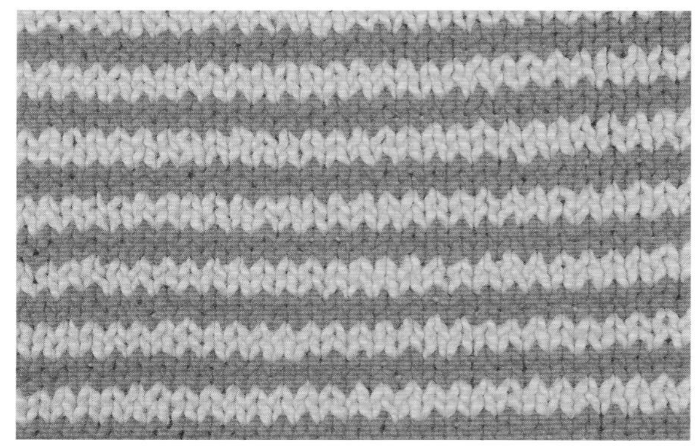

Shape Sleeve cap

Bind off 3 (4, 4) stitches at the beginning of the next four rows—43 (43, 48) stitches

Decrease row (RS) K2tog, k to last 2 sts, k2tog.

Purl one row.

Repeat the last two rows 7 (5, 6) times more—27 (31, 34) stitches.

Work three rows.

Decrease row (RS) K2tog, knit to last two stitches, k2tog.

Repeat the last four rows 0 (2, 3) times more—25 (25, 26) stitches.

Bind off four stitches at the beginning of the next two rows, then two stitches at the beginning of the next two rows—13 (13, 14) stitches.

Bind off remaining stitches.

Jil's Tip

When knitting two sides or two sleeves you can work them both at the same time using separate balls of yarn, ensuring a perfect match.

Shoulder Seams

With wrong sides facing each other, and front of sweater facing you, place stitches of back and front left shoulders on two parallel double-pointed needles. The seam will be visible on right side of sweater. Work three-needle bind off (page 40). Cut yarn and pull end through loop. Repeat for right shoulder.

Finishing

Set in sleeves. Sew side and sleeve seams. Turn under hems for body and sleeves along turning ridges, and sew in place.

Neck Edging

With crochet hook and MC, and beginning at left shoulder seam, work one row of single crochet (page 41) around neck edge. Cut yarn and pull through last single crochet loop to finish.

Weave in ends.

LESSON 10

Ribbing

Ribbing, made by alternating knit and purl stitches, is expandable and flexible so it's used on sections of a garment that need to stretch like sleeve cuffs, waistbands, and neckbands. Ribs can also be added as a design element.

Two-by-two ribbing

1. Knit and purl across the row following the pattern instructions.
2. On the next row knit the knit stitches and purl the purl stitches.

SIMPLE RIBBING

A simple rib, made by alternating knit one, purl one or knit two, purl two, is called a one-by-one rib or a two-by-two rib. But ribbing can alternate any number of stitches. Other variations include knit three, purl one (three-by-one), which makes a smooth and very elastic rib, and knit four, purl two, (four-by-two), which creates a decorative look. If you are working ribbing in a three-by-three pattern or larger, knit the first knit stitch through the back of the stitch for a smoother look. When binding off in ribbing, knit the knit stitches and purl the purls for extra elasticity.

A Yarn Over

A yarn over is an increase that creates a hole in the knitted fabric.

1. To make a yarn over on a knit row, bring the yarn around the needle from the front to the back. Then continue knitting. On the next row, you will purl into the yarn over just as if it was a stitch.
2. To make a yarn over on a purl row, bring the yarn around the needle from the back to the front. Then continue purling. On the next row, you will knit into the yarn over just as if it was a stitch.

1

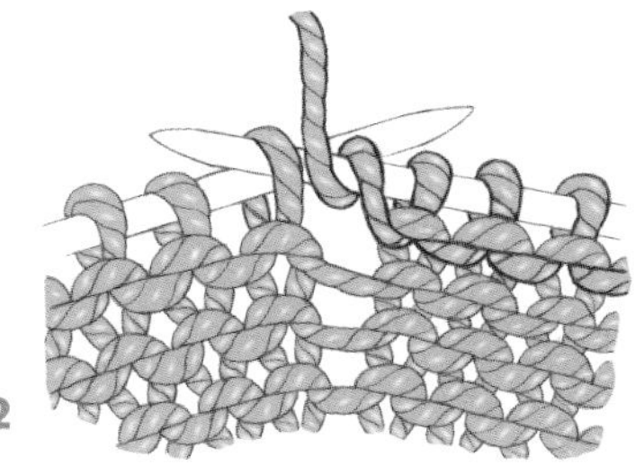

2

How to Make Yarn-Over Buttonholes

Yarn-over buttonholes, made by removing just one stitch, are

A knitted swatch with three yarn-over buttonholes

used for small buttons.

1. Work to the place you want the first buttonhole. Knit two together (page 37) through the back loops. To do this you work a k2tog but insert the needle behind the left needle into the back of the stitches.

2. Work a yarn over.

3. On the next row, purl into the yarn overs as if they were regular stitches.

Repeat these steps for each buttonhole.

How to Make a Duplicate Stitch

A bird's eye pattern consists of individual stitches in a contrasting color in an all-over design. It can be knit using two colors of working yarn, or the pattern can be worked later in duplicate stitch, which is a way to cover the original stitch with a new color. Duplicate stitch worked after each section is knit is an easy way to adorn a garment.

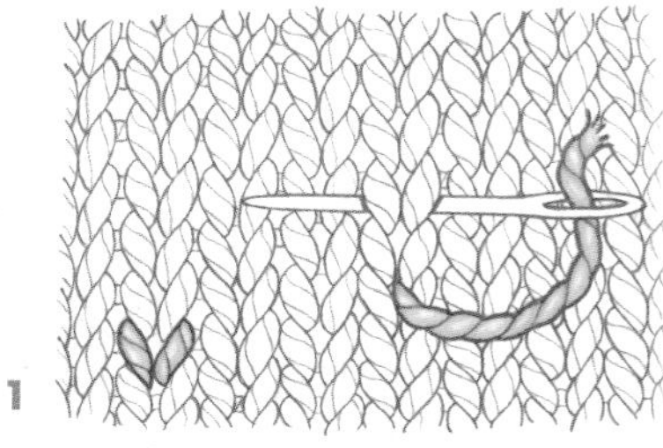

1

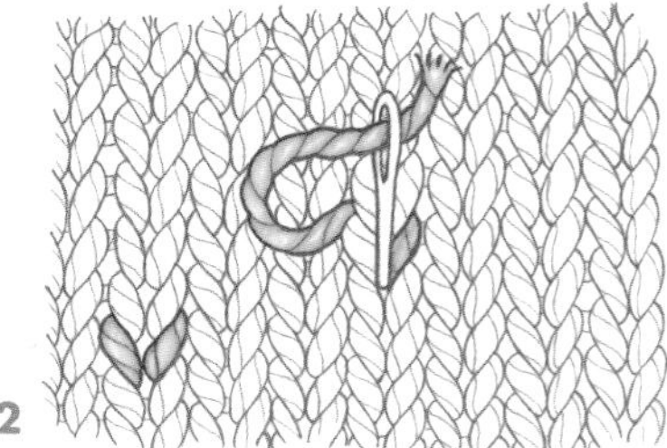

2

1. Using a tapestry needle and a contrasting color yarn, bring the needle from back to front below the stitch to be covered, and insert the needle under both loops one row above, as shown. Pull the yarn through, covering the right leg of the stitch.

2. Insert the needle back into the stitch below, covering the left leg of the stitch with the new yarn. You have now "duplicated" the stitch in a new color.

Bird's eye pattern worked in duplicate stitch

PROJECT:

bird's eye cardigan

Sample in photograph knit in Jil Eaton MinnowMerino (50g/77yds): #4793 Blue Bird (MC) and #4729 Icy Aqua (CC). Buttons from Central Yarn. Knit by Nita Young.

PROJECT:
bird's eye cardigan

This summer cardigan would be adorable in a solid color but why not create a *pièce de résistance* and add a classic bird's eye pattern with duplicate stitch. This sweater is sure to replace your child's favorite sweatshirt as the perfect cover-up for spring outings at the park or summer days at the beach.

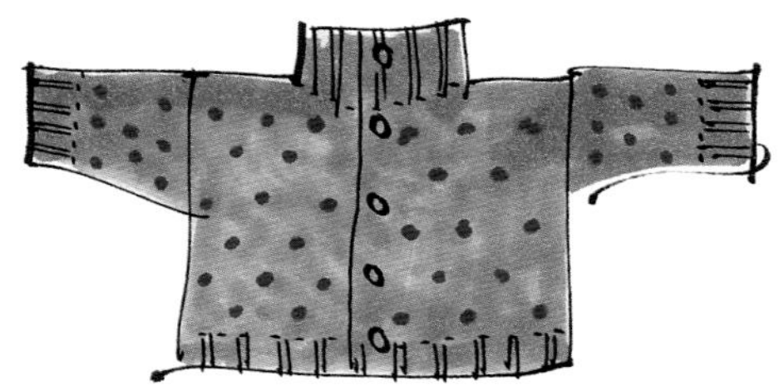

Skills

stockinette stitch .... page **46**
picking up stitches .... page **41**
three-needle bind-off.......... page **40**
yarn-over buttonholes .... page **76**
sewing a seam..................... page **37**
duplicate stitch .... page **76**

Sizes

- 1 (2, 4, 6) years
- Finished chest (buttoned) 24 (26, 28, 30)" (61 [66, 71, 76]cm)
- Finished length 11½ (12½, 14, 15)" (29 [31.5, 35.5, 38[cm)

Materials

- 330 (415, 535, 620) yards (305 [380, 490, 570]m) worsted-weight yarn (4) in MC and 30 (35, 45, 55) yards (28 [32, 42, 50]cm) in CC
- One pair size 8 (5mm) needles, *or size needed to obtain gauge*
- 3 size 8 (5mm) double-pointed needles
- 5 stitch holders
- 4 stitch markers
- One size 6 (4mm) circular needle, 16" (40.5cm) long
- Tapestry needle
- 6 buttons, ⅝" (16mm) wide

Gauge

18 stitches and 24 rows = 4" (10cm) in stockinette stitch

Stitch Pattern

K2, P1 Rib (over a multiple of 3 stitches)

Row 1 (RS) *K2, p1; repeat from * to end.

Row 2 *K1, p2; repeat from * to end.

Repeat Rows 1 and 2 for rib pattern.

Back

With straight needles and MC, cast on 54 (60, 63, 69) stitches. Work in rib pattern for four rows, end after working a wrong-side row.

Next row (RS) Knit, decrease 0 (1, 0, 1) stitch evenly across row—54 (59, 63, 68) stitches.

Beginning with a purl row, continue in stockinette stitch until piece measures 11½ (12½, 14, 15)" (29 [31.5, 35.5, 38]cm) from the beginning, end after working a wrong-side row.

Shape Shoulders and Neck

Next row (RS) K 16 (18, 19, 21) and place these stitches on holder for right shoulder, knit next 22 (23, 25, 26) stitches and place on holder for back neck, knit to end and place remaining 16 (18, 19, 21) stitches on another holder for left shoulder.

Left Front

With straight needles and MC, cast on 27 (27, 30, 33) stitches. Work in rib pattern for four rows, end after working a wrong-side row.

Next row (RS) Knit, decrease 2 (0, 0 1) stitches evenly across row—25 (27, 30, 32) stitches.

Beginning with a purl row, continue in stockinette stitch until piece measures 10 (11, 12½, 13½)" (25.5 [28, 31.5, 34.5]cm) from the beginning, end after working a right-side row.

Shape Neck and Shoulder

Bind off 5 (5, 6, 6) stitches at the next neck edge, then 2 (2, 3, 3) stitches at the next edge—18 (20, 21, 23) stitches. End after working a wrong-side row.

Decrease row (RS) Knit to last two stitches, k2tog.

Purl one row.

Repeat last two rows once more—16 (18, 19, 21) stitches.

Work even until Left Front measures same length as Back to shoulder, end after working a wrong-side row. Place stitches on holder for front left shoulder.

Right Front

Work as Left Front to neck shaping, end after working a wrong-side row.

Shape Neck and Shoulder

Bind off 5 (5, 6, 6) stitches at the next neck edge, then 2 (2, 3, 3) stitches at the next edge—18 (20, 21, 23) stitches. End after working a wrong-side row.

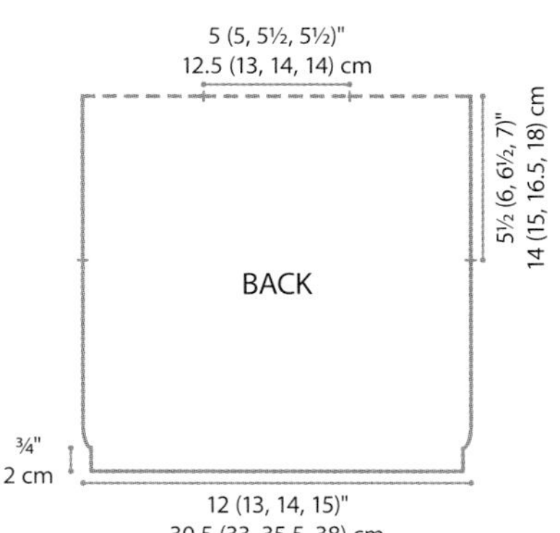

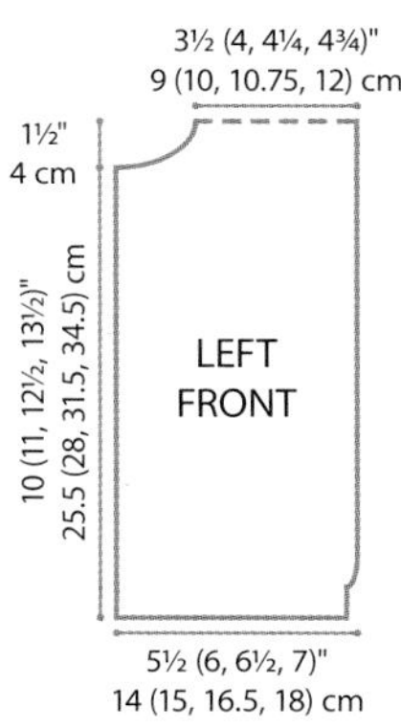

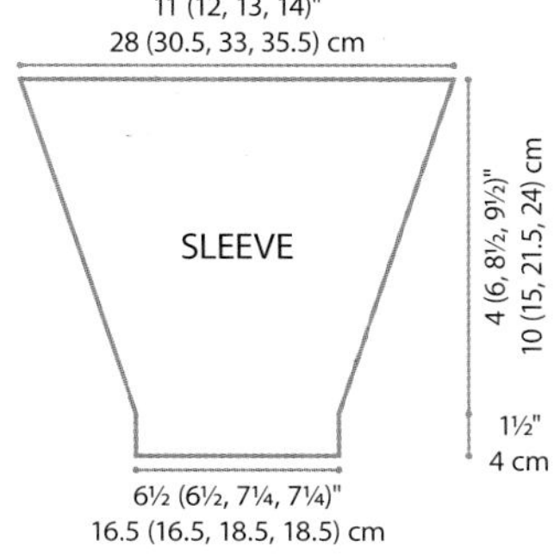

Decrease row (RS) K2tog, knit to end.

Purl one row.

Repeat last two rows once more—16 (18, 19, 21) stitches.

Work even until Right Front measures same length as Back to shoulder, end after working a wrong-side row. Place stitches on holder for front left shoulder.

Shoulder Seams

With wrong sides facing each other, and front of sweater facing you, place stitches of back and front left shoulders on two parallel double-pointed needles. Seam will be visible on right side of sweater. Work three-needle bind off (page 40). Cut yarn and pull end through loop. Repeat for right shoulder.

Jil's Tip

When binding off in ribbing, knit into the back of the knit stitches for ribbing that will stay in shape.

Sleeves

For armholes, place markers 5½ (6, 6½, 7)" (14 [15, 16.5, 18]cm) down from shoulder seams on Fronts and Back.

With right side facing, straight needles and MC, pick up and knit 50 (54, 59, 63) stitches evenly spaced between markers. Begin with a purl row, continue in stockinette stitch.

Work three rows.

Decrease row (RS) K2tog, knit to last 2 sts, k2tog.

Repeat the last four rows 0 (4, 10, 11) times more.

Purl one row.

Decrease row (RS) K2tog, knit to last 2 sts, k2tog.

Repeat the last two rows 8 (6, 1, 2) times more—30 (30, 33, 33) stitches.

Work even until piece measures 4 (6, 8½, 9½)" (10 [15, 21.5, 24]cm), end after working a wrong-side row.

Work in rib pattern for eight rows.

Bind off stitches in rib.

Finishing

Sew side and sleeve seams.

Neckband

With RS facing, circular needle and MC, begin at Right Front edge and pick up and knit 15 (14, 16, 16) stitches along neck edge, knit 22 (23, 25, 26) stitches from Back neck holder, pick up and knit 15 (14, 16, 16) stitches along the left neck—52 (51, 57, 58) stitches.

Work Row 2 of rib pattern, decreasing 1 (0, 0, 1) stitch evenly spaced—51 (51, 57, 57) stitches.

Continue in rib pattern for seven rows.

Bind off stitches in rib.

Buttonhole Band

With RS facing, straight needles and MC, begin at bottom edge of Right Front and pick up and knit 54 (59, 64, 69) stitches evenly spaced.

Beginning with Row 2, work in rib pattern for one row.

Buttonhole row (RS) Work 2 stitches in rib, *yo, k2tog, work 8 (9, 10, 11) stitches; rep from * 4 times more, end, yo, k2tog, k2.

Work two more rows in rib pattern.

Bind off stitches in rib.

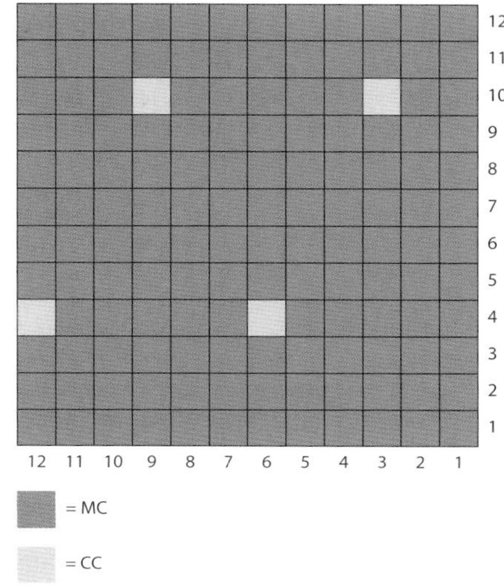

Bird's Eye Chart

Button Band

With RS facing, straight needles and MC, begin at top edge of Left Front and pick up and knit 54 (59, 64, 69) stitches evenly spaced.

Beginning with Row 2, work in rib pattern for four rows.

Bind off stitches in rib.

Sew on buttons opposite buttonholes.

Bird's Eye Pattern

With tapestry needle and CC, work bird's eye pattern in duplicate stitch on back, fronts and sleeves. Refer to Bird's Eye Chart for duplicate stitch. Do not work bird's eye pattern on ribbing.

LESSON 11

1

2

3

4

How to Make Bound-Off Buttonholes

Bound-off buttonholes can be made over two or more stitches and are used when the buttons are larger.

1. Work to the place you want the first buttonhole. Bring the yarn to the front of your work, slip the next stitch as if you were going to purl, which is called purlwise (page 37).

2. Put the yarn in back of your work and slip the next stitch purlwise again. Pass the wrapped stitch over the slipped stitched. Repeat until the necessary number of stitches have been bound off.

3. Turn the work and using the backwards loop cast-on (page 31) cast on the number of stitches you bound off, plus one.

4. Turn the work so the right side is facing, and the yarn is in back. Slip the next stitch, pass the extra stitch over that stitch, and work to the end.

Knitted swatch with three bound-off buttonholes

WHEN IN DOUBT, TEAR IT OUT!

A hole or mistake will give you grief throughout the life of the garment, but whatever time it takes to fix it now will be long forgotten. From time to time take a break and check your work: Are there mistakes or holes or dropped stitches that need to be fixed?

PROJECT:

garden party cardi

Sample in photograph knit in Rowan Kidsilk Haze (25g/229yds): #582 Trance. Buttons from Central Yarn. Knit by Donna Gross.

PROJECT:

garden party cardi

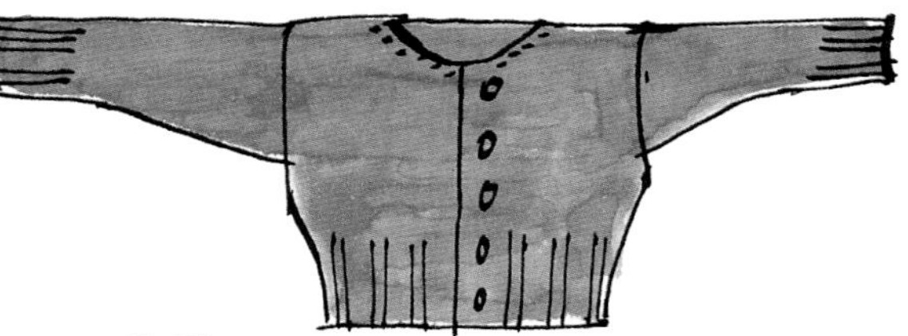

Cropped and a bit translucent, this chic cardigan is knit loosely in reverse stockinette stitch, which is the stockinette stitch with the purl side on the right side, and has matching pearl buttons. Light and airy, the yarn is a blend of featherweight mohair and silk. This stylish sweater will both delight you and charm everyone at the party!

Skills

reverse stockinette stitch ... page **46**
ribbing ... page **75**
three-needle bind-off ... page **40**
backwards loop cast-on ... page **31**
bound-off buttonholes ... page **82**
sewing a seam ... page **37**

Sizes

- S (M, L)
- Finished bust (buttoned) 35 (39, 43)" (89 [99, 109] cm)
- Finished length 17 (18, 19)" (43 [45.5, 48]cm)

Materials

- 560 (640, 730) yards (515 [590, 670]m) lightweight mohair yarn (4)
- One pair size 8 (5mm) needles, *or size needed to obtain gauge*
- 3 size 8 (5mm) double-pointed needles
- 4 stitch holders
- Tapestry needle
- 6 buttons, 7/8" (22mm) wide

Gauge

18 stitches and 28 rows = 4" (10cm) in reverse stockinette stitch

Stitch Pattern

K3, P1 Rib (over a multiple of 4 stitches + 3)

Row 1 (RS) K3, *p1, k3; repeat from * to end.

Row 2 P3, *k1, p3; repeat from * to end.

Repeat Rows 1 and 2 for rib pattern.

Back

With straight needles, cast on 79 (91, 99) stitches. Work in rib pattern for 4" (10cm), end after working a wrong-side row.

Jil's Tip

Using a contrasting smooth yarn, catch the yarn every twenty rows for easy row counting.

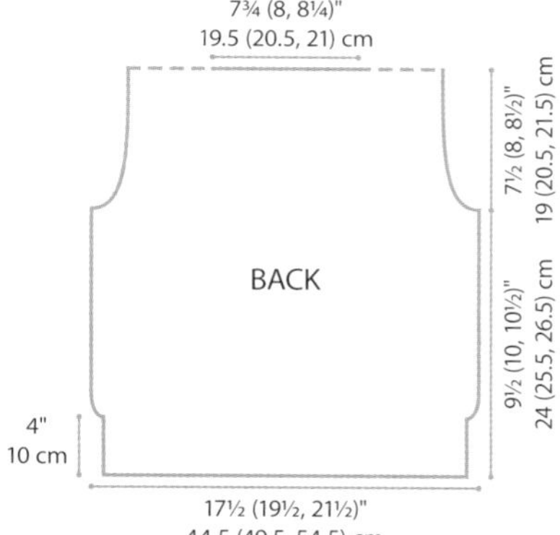

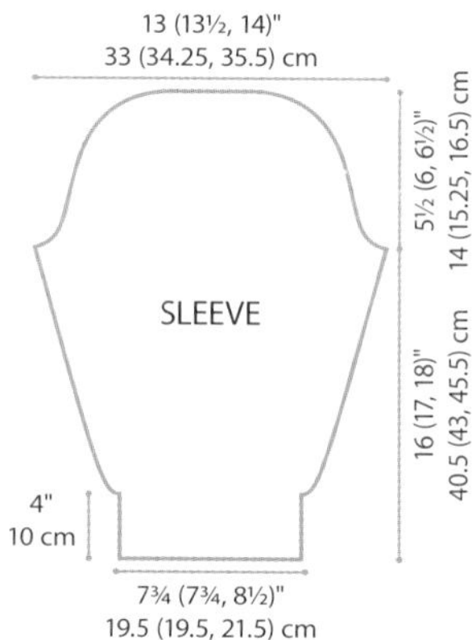

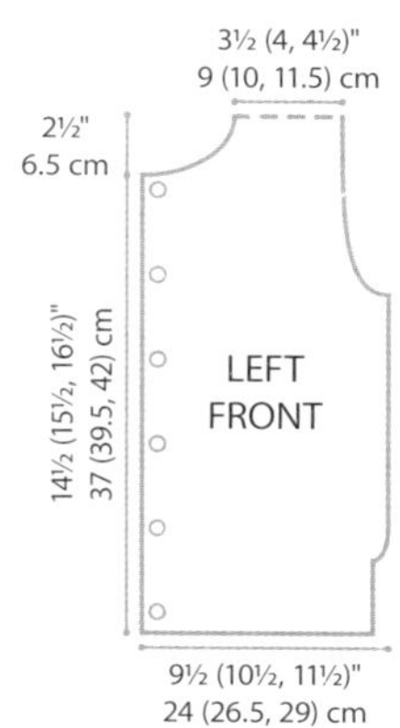

Next row (RS) Purl, decrease 0 (3, 2) stitches evenly across row—79 (88, 97) stitches.

Beginning with a knit row, continue in reverse stockinette stitch until piece measures 9½ (10, 10½)" (24 [25.5, 26.5]cm) from the beginning.

Shape Armholes

Bind off three stitches at the beginning of the next 2 (2, 4) rows, then two stitches at the beginning of the next two rows—69 (78, 81) stitches.

Decrease row (RS) P1, p2tog, purl to last 3 sts, p2tog, p1.

Knit one row.

Repeat the last two rows 0 (2, 1) times more—67 (72, 77) stitches.

Work even until armholes measure 7½ (8, 8½)" (19 [20.5, 21.5]cm), end after working a wrong-side row.

Shape Shoulders and Neck

Next row (RS) Purl 16 (18, 20) and place these stitches on holder for right shoulder, bind off next 35 (36, 37) stitches for back neck, purl to end and place remaining 16 (18, 20) stitches on another holder for left shoulder.

Left Front

With straight needles, cast on 43 (47, 51) stitches. Work in rib pattern for 4" (10cm), end after working a wrong-side row.

Next row (RS) Purl, decrease 0 (0, 1) stitch evenly across row—43 (47, 52) stitches.

Beginning with a knit row, continue in reverse stockinette stitch until piece measures same length as Back to armhole (after working a wrong-side row), shape armhole as follows.

Shape Armhole

Bind off three stitches at the beginning of the next 1 (1, 2) right-side rows, then two stitches at the beginning of the next right-side row—38 (42, 44) stitches.

Knit one row.

Decrease row (RS) P1, p2tog, purl to end.

Knit one row.

Repeat the last two rows 0 (2, 1) times more—37 (39, 42) stitches.

Work even until armhole measure 5 (5½, 6)" (12.5 [14, 15]cm), end after working a right-side row.

Shape Neck

Bind off 12 (12, 13) stitches at the next neck edge, then three stitches at the next two neck edges—19 (21, 23) stitches. End after working a wrong-side row.

Decrease row (RS) Purl to last two stitches, p2tog.

Knit one row.

Repeat last two rows twice more—16 (18, 20) stitches.

Work even until Left Front measures same length as Back to shoulder, end after working a wrong-side row. Place stitches on holder for front left shoulder.

Jil's Tip

Moving your working yarn from back to front (or vice versa) when ribbing, before taking the stitch off your needle, will increase your speed and keep your tension even.

Place markers for six buttons along front edge, with the first marker ½" (1.25cm) up from bottom edge, the last marker ¼" (.75cm) down from neck shaping, and the others spaced evenly between.

Right Front

Work as Left Front to armhole shaping, end after working a right-side row.

AT THE SAME TIME, work buttonholes opposite markers as follows.

Buttonhole row (RS) P2, bind off 2 stitches, purl to end.

Next row Cast on two stitches over the bound-off stitches using the backwards loop cast-on method (page 31).

On the next row, work these stitches through the back loops to tighten them.

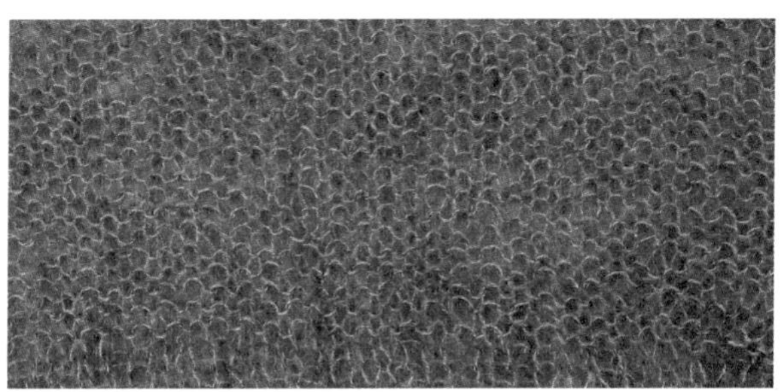

Shape Armhole

Bind off three stitches at the beginning of the next 1 (1, 2) wrong-side rows, then two stitches at the beginning of the next wrong-side row—38 (42, 44) stitches.

Decrease row (RS) Purl to last three stitches, p2tog, p1.

Knit one row.

Repeat the last two rows 0 (2, 1) times more—37 (39, 42) stitches.

Work even until armhole measure 5 (5½, 6)" (12.5 [14, 15]cm), end after working a wrong-side row.

Shape Neck

Bind off 12 (12, 13) stitches at the next neck edge, then three stitches at the next two neck edges—19 (21, 23) stitches. End after working a wrong-side row.

Decrease row (RS) P1, p2tog, purl to end.

Knit one row.

Repeat last two rows twice more—16 (18, 20) stitches.

Work even until Right Front measures same length as Back to shoulder, end after working a wrong-side row. Place stitches on holder for front left shoulder.

Sleeves

With straight needles, cast on 35 (35, 39) stitches. Work in rib pattern for 4" (10cm), end after working a wrong-side row.

Continue in reverse stockinette stitch and purl one row.

Increase row (WS) K1, increase in next stitch, knit to last two stitches, increase in next stitch, k1.

Work seven rows.

Increase row (WS) K1, increase in next stitch, knit to last two stitches, increase in next stitch, k1.

Repeat the last eight rows 0 (1, 6) times more.

Work five rows.

Increase row (WS) K1, increase in next stitch, knit to last two stitches, increase in next stitch, k1.

Repeat the last six rows 9 (9, 3) times more—59 (61, 63) stitches.

Work even until piece measures 16 (17, 18)" (40.5 [43, 45.5]cm) from the beginning, end after working a wrong-side row.

Shape Sleeve Cap

Bind off three stitches at the beginning of the next 2 (2, 4) rows, then two stitches at the beginning of the next two rows—49 (51, 47) stitches.

For Small Size Only

Decrease row (RS) P1, p2tog, purl to last three stitches, p2tog, p1.

Decrease row K1, k2tog, knit to last three stitches, k2tog, k1.

Decrease row P1, p2tog, purl to last three stitches, p2tog, p1—43 stitches.

For Medium and Large Sizes Only

Decrease row (RS) P1, p2tog, purl to last three stitches, p2tog, p1—49 (45) stitches.

For All Sizes

Knit one row.

Decrease row (RS) P1, p2tog, purl to last three stitches, p2tog, p1.

Repeat the last two rows 12 (15, 10) times more—17 (17, 23) stitches.

For Large Size Only

Work three rows.

Decrease row (RS) P1, p2tog, purl to last 3 sts, p2tog, p1.

Repeat the last four rows twice more—17 stitches.

For All Sizes

Knit one row.

Bind off two stitches at beginning of next four rows—9 stitches.

Bind off.

Shoulder Seams

With wrong sides facing each other, and front of sweater facing you, place stitches of back and front left shoulders on two parallel double-pointed needles. Seam will be visible on right side of sweater. Work three-needle bind-off (page 40). Cut yarn and pull end through loop. Repeat for right shoulder.

Finishing

Neckband

With right side facing, pick up and knit 83 (83, 87) stitches evenly around neck edge. Work in rib pattern for three rows. Bind off stitches in rib.

Set in sleeves.

Sew side and sleeve seams.

Sew buttons on left front at markers.

Jil's Tip

Working the first and last stitch in a row in Stockinette Stitch will make the seam smooth and picking up stitches will be easy.

LESSON 12

1

3

How to Make Cables

Cables are a fun and easy way to add texture to your knitting. You make a cable by placing a number of stitches on a short cable needle and holding them either in front or in back of your work. You knit stitches from the left needle, then knit the stitches on the cable needle. Cables make a beautiful fabric that looks complicated, but is not.

1. For this Cable Back Six (CB6) pattern work to the first cable. Slip three stitches onto the cable needle and hold in back of the work.
2. Knit the next three stitches from your left needle.
3. Then pull your cable needle over to the front and knit the stitches from the cable needle.
4. Continue to the next cable and repeat.

Work the cable row every eight rows on the right side. Don't worry that stitches seem tightly pulled when you work from the cable needle. As you continue knitting these stitches will gently fall into place.

Cable back six

LEFT AND RIGHT CABLES

The simplest cables to knit are those where three or more stitches are placed on a cable needle. Holding the stitches to the back, as described here, creates a right crossing cable; holding the stitches to the front creates a left crossing cable.

How to Make a Tassel

I love tassels and pompoms that are thick and are sewn on tightly, for a perky effect. The more yarn you use, the thicker the tassel will be.

1. Cut two eight-inch (20.5cm) strands of yarn and set aside. Wrap the yarn around your fingers seventy times. Remove your fingers and pull the first strand through the bundle. Wrap it around twice and tie it tightly.

2. Wrap the second strand around twice, one inch (2.5 cm) down from the top, and tie it tightly.

3. Cut the loops at the other end and trim evenly. Use the first strand to tie the tassel tightly to the knitted garment.

A simple-to-make tassel adds just the right note to this colorful cap (page 115).

PROJECT:

big fish little fishie

A classic fully-cabled pullover for the big fish and a matching baby hat for the little fishie make a captivating duo. Worked in a bulky weight wool blend for cozy warmth, they are just the right weight for cool days any time of the year. These stylish QuickKnits™ stitch up in a jiffy.

Skills

stockinette stitch .... page **46**
cables .... page **88**
three-needle bind-off .... page **40**
picking up stitches .... page **41**
sewing a seam .... page **37**
tassels .... page **89**

Big Fish Sweater

Sizes

- S (M, L, XL)
- Finished chest 40 (44 1/2, 49, 52)" (101.5 [113, 124.5, 132]cm)
- Finished length 25½ (26½, 27¼, 28)" (64.5 [67.5, 69, 71]cm)

Gauge

24 stitches and 24 rows = 4" (10cm) in Sweater Cable Pattern

Jil's Tip

Sew seams of knits made of bulky yarns with a finer yarn in the same color.

Materials

- 1455 (1615, 1740, 1870) yards (1335 [1480, 1595, 1710]m) heavy worsted-weight yarn (5)
- One pair size 9 (5.5mm) needles, *or size needed to obtain gauge*
- Cable needle
- 3 size 8 (5mm) double-pointed needles
- One size 9 (5.5mm) circular needle, 16" (40.5cm) long
- 4 stitch holders
- 4 stitch markers
- Tapestry needle

Samples in photograph knit in Classic Elite Yarns Montera (100g/127yds): #3803 Falcon Gray. Sweater knit by Mark Dube and Donna Gross. Hat knit by Jil Eaton.

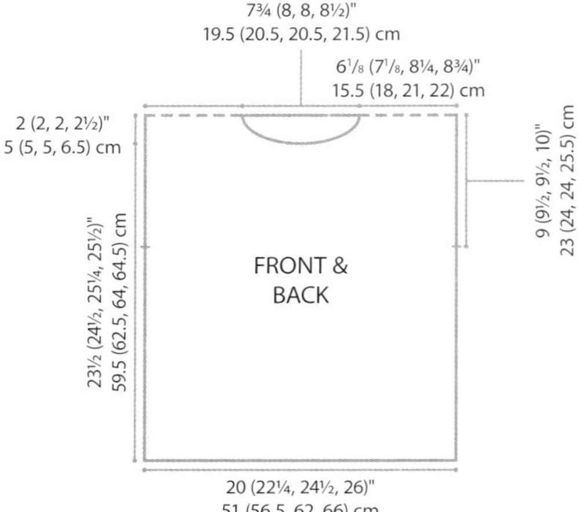

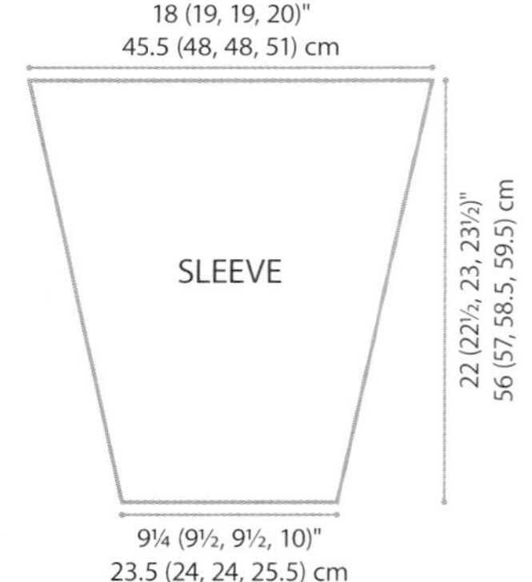

Stitch Pattern

Sweater Cable Pattern (over a multiple of 7 stitches +1)

Rows 1, 3, and 7 (RS) P1, *k6, p1; repeat from * to end.

Rows 2, 4, and 6 K1, *p6, k1; repeat from * to end.

Row 5 P1, *slip three stitches to cable needle and hold to back of work, k3, k3 from cable needle, p1; repeat from * to end.

Row 8 As Row 2.

Repeat Rows 1–8 for Sweater Cable Pattern.

Back

With straight needles, cast on 120 (134, 148, 155) stitches. Beginning with Row 1, work in Sweater Cable Pattern until piece measures 25½ (26½, 27¼, 28)" (64.5 [67.5, 69, 71]cm) from the beginning, end after working a wrong-side row.

Shape Shoulders and Neck

Next row (RS) K 37 (43, 50, 52) and place stitches on a holder for back right shoulder, bind off next 46 (48, 48, 51) stitches knitwise for back neck, knit to end and place remaining 37 (43, 50, 52) stitches on another holder for back left shoulder.

Front

Work as Back until piece measures 23½ (24½, 25¼, 25½)" (59.5 [62.5, 64, 64.5]cm) from the beginning, end after working a wrong-side row.

Shape Right Neck and Shoulder

Next row (RS) Work 48 (55, 62, 65) stitches, place remaining 75 (79, 86, 90) stitches on holder. Turn.

Next row (WS) Bind off four stitches, work to end—44 (51, 58, 61) stitches.

Work one row.

Next row (WS) Bind off three stitches, work to end—41 (48, 55, 58) stitches.

Repeat last two rows once more—38 (45, 52, 55) stitches.

Next row (RS) Work to last two stitches, k2tog.

Work one row.

Repeat the last two rows 0 (1, 1, 2) times more—37 (43, 50, 52) stitches.

Work even, if necessary, until Front measures same length as Back to shoulder, end after working a wrong-side row. Place stitches on holder.

Shape Left Neck and Shoulder

With right side facing, place stitches on holder back to left needle, ready for a right-side row.

Next row (RS) Join yarn and bind off center 24 (24, 24, 25) stitches, work to end—48 (55, 62, 65) stitches.

Work one row.

Next row (RS) Bind off 4 stitches, work to end—44 (51, 58, 61) stitches.

Work one row.

Next row (RS) Bind off three stitches, work to end—41 (48, 55, 58) stitches.

Repeat last two rows once more—38 (45, 52, 55) stitches.

Work one row.

Next row (RS) K2tog, work to end.

Work one row.

Repeat the last two rows 0 (1, 1, 2) times more—37 (43, 50, 52) stitches.

Work even, if necessary, until Front measures same length as Back to shoulder, end after working a wrong-side row. Place stitches on holder.

Shoulder Seams

With wrong sides facing each other, and front of sweater facing you, place stitches of back and front left shoulders on two parallel double pointed needles. Seam will be visible on right side of sweater. Work three-needle bind-off (page 40). Cut yarn and pull end through loop. Repeat for right shoulder.

Sleeves

For armholes, place markers 9 (9½, 9½, 10)" (23 [24, 24, 25.5]cm) down from shoulder seams on Front and Back.

With right side facing and straight needles, pick up and knit 106 (113, 113, 120) stitches evenly spaced between markers.

Begin Sweater Cable Pattern with Row 2.

Work four rows.

Decrease row (RS) K2tog, knit to last two stitches, k2tog.

Work five rows.

Decrease row (RS) K2tog, knit to last two stitches, k2tog.

Repeat last six rows 11 (7, 8, 6) times more.

Work three rows.

Decrease row (RS) K2tog, knit to last 2 sts, k2tog.

Repeat last four rows 11 (18, 17, 21) times more —56 (57, 57, 60) stitches.

Work even until piece measures 22 (22½, 23, 23½)" (56 [57, 58.5, 59.5]cm). Bind off stitches in cable pattern.

Finishing

Neckband

With right side facing and circular needle, begin at left shoulder seam and pick up and knit 8 (8, 8, 10) stitches along left neck edge, 16 stitches across front neck, 8 (8, 8, 10) stitches along right neck edge, and 31 (32, 32, 34) stitches across back neck—63 (64, 64, 70) stitches. Join and place marker for beginning of rounds. Knit eight rounds. Bind off stitches loosely and evenly.

Sew side and sleeve seams. Weave in ends.

Little Fishie Hat

Sizes

- Newborn to 3 months (6 months, 1 year, 2 years)
- Finished circumference 14½ (15½, 16¾, 17¾)" (36.5 [39.5, 42.5, 45]cm)

Materials

- 95 (100, 125, 130) yards (90 [95, 115, 120]m) heavy worsted-weight yarn (5)
- One pair size 9 (5.5mm) needles, or size needed to obtain gauge
- Cable needle
- Tapestry needle

Gauge

24 stitches and 24 rows = 4" (10cm) in hat cable pattern

Stitch Pattern

Hat Cable Pattern (over a multiple of 7 stitches +2)

Rows 1, 3 and 7 (RS) *P1, k6; repeat from *, end p2.

Rows 2, 4, and 6 K2, *p6, k1; repeat from * to end.

Row 5 *P1, slip 3 stitches to cable needle and hold to back of work, k3, k3 from cable needle; repeat from *, end p2.

Row 8 As for Row 2.

Repeat Rows 1–8 for Hat Cable Pattern.

Hat

Cast on 66 (73, 80, 87) stitches. Work in stockinette stitch for five rows.

Increase row (WS) Purl and increase 20 stitches evenly across—86 (93, 100, 107) stitches.

Repeat rows 1–8 of Hat Cable Pattern 3 (3, 4, 4) times, then work Row 1 once more. Piece should measure approximately 5 (5, 6¼, 6¼)" (12.5 [12.5, 16, 16]cm) from the beginning.

Shape Crown

Row 1 (WS) K2, *p2tog, p2, p2tog, k1; repeat from * across—62 (67, 72, 77) stitches.

Rows 2 and 3 Knit the knit stitches and purl the purl stitches, as they face you.

Row 4 (RS) *P1, slip 2 stitches to cable needle and hold to back of work, k2, k2 from cable needle; repeat from *, end p2.

Row 5 K2, *p2tog twice, k1; repeat from * to end—38 (41, 44, 47) stitches.

Row 6 As for Row 2.

Row 7 K2, *p2tog, k1; repeat from * to end—26 (28, 30, 32) stitches.

Row 8 (RS) K2tog across—13 (14, 15, 16) stitches.

Row 9 P2tog across, end p 1 (0, 1, 0) —7 (7, 8, 8) stitches.

Cut yarn leaving a long tail and pull through remaining stitches. Use the tail to sew the back seam of the hat, reversing the seam at the stockinette stitch rolled edge.

Tassel

Make a tassel (page 89) and use the strand that secured the bundle to tie the tassel tightly to the top of the hat so that it stands straight up.

LESSON 13

Knitting lace

Jil's Tip
To make knitting lace easier, use bamboo or wood needles to avoid slippage, and choose needles with long graceful points.

How to Knit Lace

Knitting lace is simple—you make a series of yarn-over loops and decreases that create an openwork pattern. Even so, it is considered the height of the art of knitting, and no education in the craft would be complete without it. Lace is often misunderstood as complicated and time consuming, but many lace patterns are actually very easy and knit up quickly. You have to follow the directions carefully in the beginning, but after a few rows you will have the pattern in your head and the work will go quickly.

If you are just beginning to knit a lace pattern you might want to find a pattern that has one or more rows of even knitting in between the lace pattern; this will also make things much simpler should you have to pull back to fix a mistake. Commonly patterns are made from yarn overs (yo's), but you can also work a slip one, knit one, pass slipped stitch over (skpsso). Be careful not to stretch your slipped stitches, as that can result in an uneven or baggy lace pattern.

Lace patterns can be written out, worked from a chart, or both. Read through your pattern completely to make sure you understand everything you need to do for that particular design. I also recommend enlarging your chart; you can then tick off the rows as you knit them, helping to keep your place.

GETTING YOUR GAUGE

When making a gauge swatch, getting the correct number of stitches per inch (centimeter) is more important than getting the row count. If your row count is off, however, you run the risk of running out of yarn. Consider buying another ball of yarn if the row count is off.

PROJECT:
la petite shrug

Sample in photograph knit in Blue Sky Alpacas Alpaca Silk (50g/146yds): #141 Peapod. Knit by Donna Gross.

PROJECT:

la petite shrug

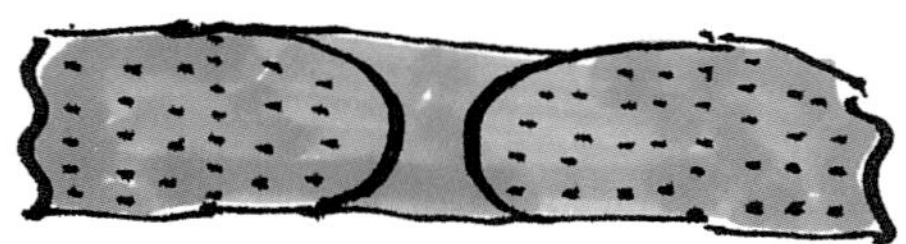

Just right for day or night, this sophisticated shoulder shrug will take you from work to dinner out with elegance and style. The graceful design has an eyelet effect, making the garment light and airy, perfect for wearing almost anywhere you go.

Skills

stockinette stitch .... page **46**
three-needle bind-off.......... page **40**
yarn over............................. page **75**

Sizes

- XS (S, M, L)
- Finished width (cuff to cuff) 26 (29, 32, 35)" (66 [73.5, 81, 89]cm)
- Finished back length 11½ (11½, 13, 14¼)" (29 [29, 33, 36]cm)

Materials

- 325 (365, 455, 545) yards (300 [355, 420, 500]m) sportweight (2)
- One size 5 (3.75mm) circular needle, 16" (40.5cm) long, *or size needed to obtain gauge*
- 3 size 8 (5mm) double pointed needles
- Stitch marker
- Tapestry needle

Gauge

31 stitches and 28 rows = 4" (10cm) in lace patterns

Stitch Patterns

Circular Lace Pattern (multiple of 10 stitches)

Round 1 Knit.

Round 2 *K1, yo, k3, sl1, k2tog, psso, k3, yo; rep from * around.

Repeat rounds 1 and 2 for Circular Lace Pattern.

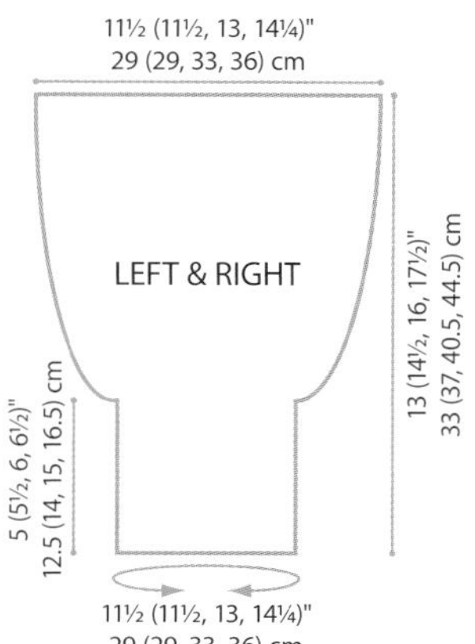

Straight Lace Pattern (multiple of 10 stitches +1)

Row 1 (WS) Purl.

Row 2 (RS) K1, *yo, k3, sl1, k2tog, psso, k3, yo, k1; rep from * to end.

Repeat Rows 1 and 2 for Straight Lace Pattern.

Left Half

Sleeve

Cast on 90 (90, 100, 110) stitches. Join, being careful not to twist stitches on needle, and place marker for beginning of round.

Work in Circular Lace Pattern until piece measures 5 (5½, 6, 6½)" (12.5 [14, 15, 16.5]cm) from the beginning, end after working Round 2, and cast on one stitch at the end of this round—91 (91, 101, 111) stitches.

Divide for Body

Remove marker and begin working back and forth in Straight Lace Pattern until piece measures 13 (14½, 16, 17½)" (33 [37, 40.5, 44.5]cm) from the beginning, end after working a right-side row. Place stitches on a double-pointed needle.

Right Half

Work as for Left Half.

Back Seam

With right sides facing each other, hold stitches of left and right halves on two parallel double-pointed needles. Binding off stitches loosely, work three-needle bind-off (page 40). Cut yarn and pull end through loop.

Finishing

Weave in ends.

graduate school

Now we can get serious! These final projects will expand your knitting repertoire as you learn how to knit a Fair Isle design, turn a heel, and create textured stitch patterns. Are you up for the challenge? There are so many myths about knitting, most of which say that these techniques are difficult to accomplish. But if you simply slow down and follow the instructions one step at a time, the heel will appear like magic and the textured pattern will take shape before your eyes. Learning new techniques takes patience, but if you persevere, you will be thrilled with your work and become a knitter for life.

PROJECT INDEX

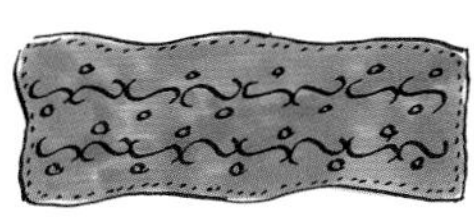

LESSON 14

1

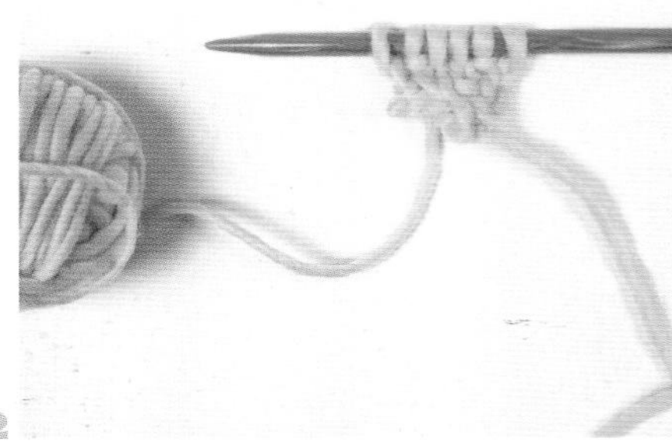
2

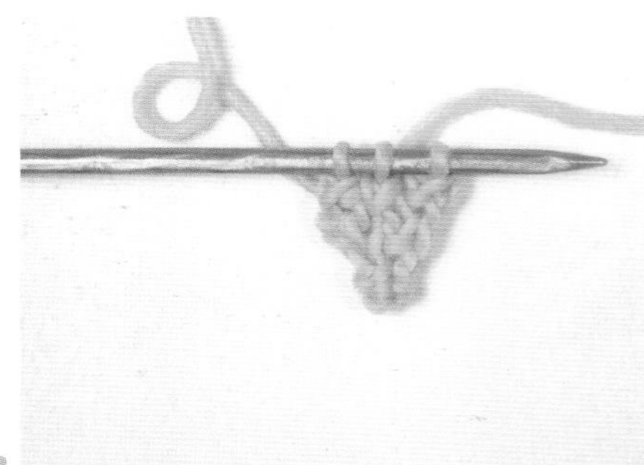
3

4

How to Make Knit-In Bobbles

A bobble, a design detail usually worked in stockinette stitch, is a three-dimensional shape made by increasing in a stitch, working a few rows, and then decreasing back to the original stitch. Bobbles can be made separately (as shown here) and sewn on later during finishing, or they can be knit right in the piece as is done in the Bobble Shawl, opposite.

1. Begin with one stitch on the needle, or if you are making the bobble as you knit, work to where you want the bobble to be. Increase: knit in the front and the back, and again in the front and the back, making four stitches out of one.

2. If you are making the bobble as you knit, slip the stitches back on to the left needle. Bring the yarn across the back and knit the four stitches. Repeat this four-stitch row three more times.

3. Pass the second stitch over the first, the third over the second, and the fourth over the third.

4. If you are making the bobble separately, cut the yarn, leaving a six-inch (15cm) tail, and pull the tail through the remaining stitch on the needle to fasten off.

Five bobbles worked in stockinette stitch

PROJECT:
bobble shawl

Sample in photograph knit in Classic Elite Yarns Waterlily (50g/100yds): #1947 Lake. Knit by Donna Gross.

PROJECT:
bobble shawl

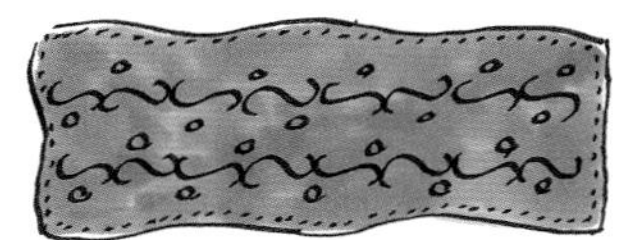

A generous shawl adorned with cables and bobbles, this wrap is destined to become an heirloom. Warm and thick, the shawl makes a glamorous cover-up for brisk evenings, as well as a lovely lap robe when you are sitting all cozy by the fire.

Skills

stockinette stitch .... page **46**
reverse stockinette stitch.... page **46**
cables .... page **88**
bobbles .... page **102**

Finished Size

25" (63.5cm) wide by 63" (160cm) long

Gauge

18 stitches and 24 rows = 4" (10cm) in stockinette stitch

17 stitches = 2¾" (7cm) in cable panel

Materials

- 1,770 yards (1620m) worsted-weight yarn (4)
- One size 8 (8mm) circular needle, 40" (101.5cm) long, *or size needed to obtain gauge*
- Cable needle
- 6 Stitch markers
- Tapestry needle

Jil's Tip

If your needle has slipped out entirely, use a circular needle to pick up the stitches so you won't have to worry about the direction of the needle.

Pattern Notes

4-RPC (4-st right purl cable) Slip one stitch to cable needle and hold to back, k3, p1 from cable needle.

5-RPC (5-st right purl cable) Slip two stitches to cable needle and hold to back, k3, p2 from cable needle.

5-LPC (5-st left purl cable) Slip three stitches to cable needle and hold to front, p2, k3 from cable needle.

7-RC (7-st right cable) Slip four stitches to cable needle and hold to back, k3, slip p stitch from cable needle to left-hand needle and p1, k3 from cable needle.

MB (make bobble) Knit into front, back, front, and back of stitch (four stitches made in one stitch), turn, p4, turn, k4, turn, p2tog twice, turn, k2tog.

Stitch Pattern

Cable Panel (over 17 stitches)

Row 1 (WS) P1 tbl, k4, p3, k1, p3, k4, p1 tbl.

Row 2 (RS) K1 tbl, p4, 7-RC, p4, k1 tbl.

Row 3 and all following WS rows P1 tbl, knit the knit stitches and purl the purl stitches as they face you to last stitch, end p1 tbl.

Row 4 K1 tbl, p2, 5-RPC, p1, 5-LPC, p2, k1 tbl.

Row 6 K1 tbl, p2, k3, p2, MB, p2, k3, p2, k1 tbl.

Row 8 K1 tbl, p9, 4-RPC, p2, k1 tbl.

Row 10 K1 tbl, p8, 4-RPC, p3, k1 tbl.

Row 12 K1 tbl, p7, 4-RPC, p4, k1 tbl.

Row 14 K1 tbl, p6, 4-RPC, p5, k1 tbl.

Row 16 K1 tbl, p5, 4-RPC, p6, k1 tbl.

Row 18 K1 tbl, p4, 4-RPC, p7, k1 tbl.

Row 20 K1 tbl, p3, 4-RPC, p8, k1 tbl.

Row 22 K1 tbl, p2, 4-RPC, p4, k3, p2, k1 tbl.

Row 24 As Row 6.

Row 26 K1 tbl, p2, 5-LPC, p1, 5-RPC, p2, k1 tbl.

Repeat Rows 1–26 for Cable Panel.

Shawl

Cast on 113 stitches. Work in stockinette stitch for eight rows.

Next row (RS) Purl for bottom turning ridge.

Purl one row.

Continue in stockinette stitch for six more rows.

Next row (RS) Cast on six stitches, knit these six stitches, knit to end, increasing 22 stitches evenly across, cast on six stitches—147 stitches.

Establish Pattern

Next row (WS) P5, k1 (1 stitch in reverse stockinette stitch for side turning ridge), p5, pm (, [work Row 1 of Cable Panel over next seventeen stitches, PM, work ten stitches in stockinette stitch, pm] four times, work Row 1 of Cable Panel over next seventeen stitches, pm, p5, k1 (1 stitch in reverse stockinette stitch for side turning ridge), p5.

Continue in pattern as established and work Rows 2–26 of Cable Panel once, and then repeat Rows 1–26 thirteen times more. Piece should measure approximately 62" (157.5cm) from bottom turning ridge.

Next row (WS) Bind off six stitches, purl to last six stitches, decreasing 22 stitches evenly across—119 stitches.

Next row Bind off six stitches, knit to end—113 stitches.

Continue in stockinette stitch for five more rows.

Next row (WS) Knit for top turning ridge.

Knit one row.

Continue in stockinette stitch for seven more rows. Bind off stitches.

Finishing

Turn under top and bottom hems at turning ridges and sew in place. Repeat for side hems.

LESSON 15

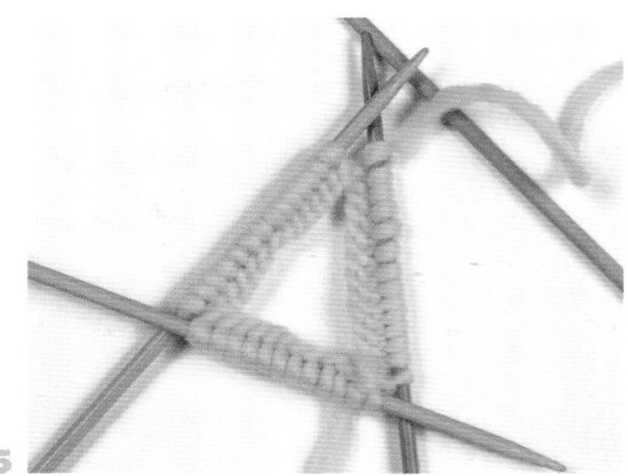

5

Jil's Tip

If you're just beginning to work with double-pointed needles, working over a table will make it easier to support them.

How to Use Double-Pointed Needles

When knitting in the round on a circumference too small for a circular needle we use four, or sometimes five, double-pointed needles (dpns). Socks, hats, and gloves are all worked on double-pointed needles. The first few rows can be tricky, balancing the needles, but after a few rounds you'll be surprised how easy it is. Always pull the first two stitches tighter than normal to prevent unattractive loose stitches, called laddering, at the beginning of the rounds.

1. Cast on the number of stitches needed for the first needle plus one.

2. Place the last stitch on the next needle, and cast on the number needed plus one again.

3. Place the last stitch on the third needle, and cast on the remaining number of stitches.

4. Making sure not to twist your stitches, lay the needles out in a triangle on a flat surface, with the cast-on edge pointing in, as shown.

5. With your free needle, knit the first stitch, then place a row marker and work to the end. Continue knitting the stitches on each needle to finish the round.

WORKING WITH FUZZY YARN

Place fuzzy yarn such as mohair or any light colored yarn in a large zip-loc plastic bag to keep the yarn clean as you knit. If you need to rip out your work in mohair, placing the item in the freezer for a few hours will make ripping out easier. Really!

How to Make a Sock

Socks may look complicated but they are really quite simple if you follow the directions step by step. It helps if you know the knitting terms used for the parts of the sock and in what order to knit them.

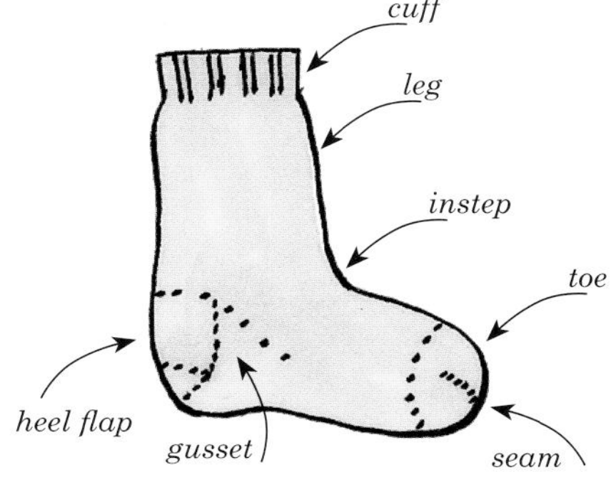

1. Knit the cuff and leg on double-pointed needles (page 106).
2. Knit the heel flap.
3. Turn the heel by making short rows and wrapping the end stitch (page 108).
4. Pick up stitches for the gusset.
5. Knit the instep.
6. Knit the foot.
7. Decrease for the toe.
8. Seam the toe (page 108).

How to Turn a Heel

I remember the first time I knit a sock, and turned the heel—it felt like magic! Turning a heel is actually shaping using a short row technique. Short rows are partial rows of knitting, where you knit some of the stitches on a row but not all of them, resulting in shaping without any decreasing of stitches. To prevent holes at the end of the short rows you must wrap the last stitch.

Turning a heel, shown from the bottom of the heel

Jil's Tip
I use bamboo needles for knitting socks because the yarn is less likely to slip.

Turning a heel, shown from the front

How to Wrap a Stitch

On short rows, you wrap the last stitch before turning to prevent holes.

1. Work the number of stitches called for in the pattern.
2. With the yarn in back, slip the next stitch purlwise.
3. Move the yarn between the needles to the front of the work.
4. Slip the slipped stitch back onto the original needle and turn your work.

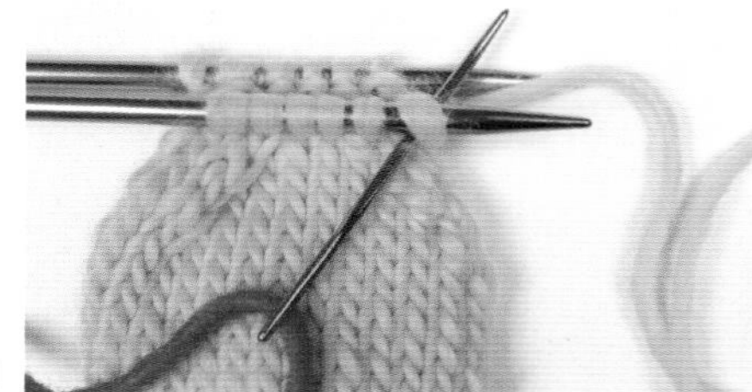
1

How to Do the Kitchener Stitch

The Kitchener stitch is a way of grafting two pieces of knitting together without a seam. Smooth, seamless, and comfortable to wear, it's the ideal method for seaming sock toes.

1. Hold the two pieces together in your left hand with the wrong sides facing and the needles parallel. With a length of the yarn threaded on a tapestry needle, put the needle through the first stitch on the front knitting needle as if to knit and slip it off the needle.
2. Put the needle into the second stitch on the front knitting needle as if to purl and leave it on the needle.
3. Pull to tighten, and put the needle into the first stitch on the back knitting needle as if to purl and slip off needle.
4. Put the needle into the second stitch on the back knitting needle as if to knit and leave it on the needle. Pull to tighten, and repeat these steps until all the stitches are off the knitting needles.

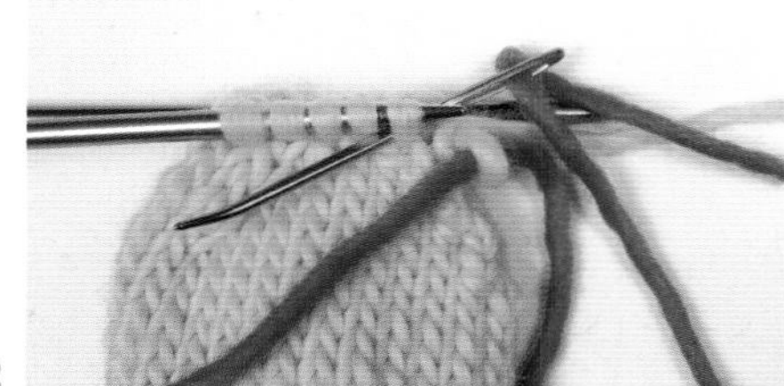
2

3

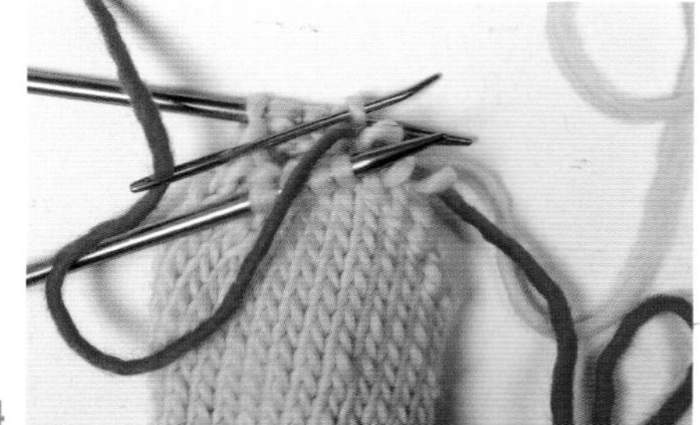
4

PROJECT:

toasty toes

Samples in photograph knit in Classic Elite Yarns Lush (50g/124yds): #4457 Blueberry and #4458 Lipstick. Knit by Stephanie Doben.

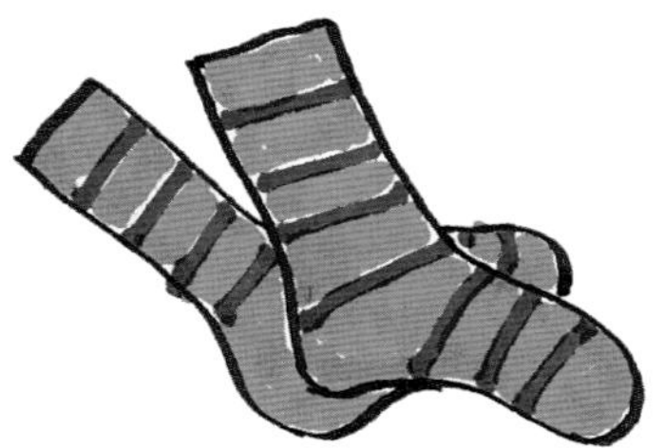

PROJECT:

toasty toes

Perky striped boot socks for kids and adults make marvelous gifts—they knit up quickly and are extremely wearable. Everyone's toes will be toasty warm inside boots or skates, and these socks make comfy slipper socks *après-ski*, too.

Skills

knitting on double-pointed needles .... page **106**
turning a heel .... page **107**
kitchener stitch .... page **108**

Sizes

- Toddler (Child, Adult Small, Adult Medium, Adult Large)
- Finished length (heel to toe) 5 (7½, 9, 10, 11)" (12.5 [19, 23, 25.5, 28]cm)

Materials

- 70 (125, 170, 215, 250) yards (65 [115, 160, 200, 230]m) worsted-weight yarn (4) in MC, and 15 (25, 30, 45, 55) yards (15 [25, 30, 45, 50]m) in CC
- One set of 4 size 7 (4.5mm) double-pointed needles, *or size needed to obtain gauge*
- Stitch marker
- Tapestry needle

Gauge

20 stitches and 32 rows = 4" (10cm) in pattern stitch

Stitch Pattern

Stripe Pattern (worked in the round)

Rounds 1–4 Knit with MC.

Round 5 Knit with CC.

Round 6 Purl with CC.

Rounds 7–10 Knit with MC.

Repeat Rounds 1–10 for Stripe Pattern.

Top

With MC, cast on 28 (32, 36, 40, 44) stitches and distribute on three needles as follows: 8-12-8 (12-8-12, 12-12-12, 12-16-12, 16-12-16). Join, being careful not to twist stitches, and place marker at beginning of round.

Work in the round in k2, p2 rib for 1 (1½, 2, 2, 2½)" (2.5 [4, 5, 5, 6.5]cm).

Work in Stripe Pattern for 2½ (4, 5, 6, 6)" (6.5 [10, 12.5, 15, 15]cm).

Cut CC and continue with MC only.

Heel Flap

Next round (divide for heel) Knit 7 (8, 9, 10, 11) stitches from first needle for heel; without working, place next 14 (16, 18, 20, 22) stitches on two needles for instep; slip last 7 (8, 9, 10, 11) stitches onto first needle for heel.

Work back and forth on 14 (16, 18, 20, 22) heel stitches as follows:

Row 1 (WS) Slip 1 purlwise with yarn in back, purl to end.

Row 2 *Slip 1 purlwise with yarn in back, bring yarn to front and p1; repeat from * to end.

Repeat last 2 rows for 1 (1½, 2, 2½, 2½)" (2.5 [4, 5, 6.5, 6.5]cm) for heel flap, end after working Row 2.

Turning the Heel

Row 1 (WS) Slip 1, p 6 (8, 8, 10, 10), p2tog, p1, turn.

Row 2 Slip 1, k 1 (3, 1, 3, 1), ssk, k1, turn.

Row 3 Slip 1, p 2 (4, 2, 4, 2), p2tog, p1, turn.

Row 4 Slip 1, k 3 (5, 3, 5, 3), ssk, k1, turn.

Row 5 Slip 1, p 4 (6, 4, 6, 4), p2tog, p1, turn.

Row 6 Slip 1, k 5, (7, 5, 7, 5), ssk, k1, turn—8 (10, 12, 14, 16) stitches.

For Adult Small, Medium, and Large Only

Row 7 Slip 1, p 6 / 8 / 6, p2tog, k1, turn.

Row 8 Slip 1, k 7 / 9 / 7, ssk, k1—8 (10,12, 14) stitches.

For Adult Large Only

Row 9 Slip 1, p 8, p2tog, p1, turn.

Row 10 Slip 1, k9, ssk, k1—12 stitches remain.

Instep and Foot

Place 14 (16, 18, 20, 22) instep stitches on one needle (Needle 2). Begin working in rounds again and resume stripe pattern.

With right side facing and MC, pick up and knit 6 (9, 11, 14, 14) stitches along right edge of heel flap (Needle 1); knit across Needle 2; pick up and knit 6 (9, 11, 14, 14) stitches along left edge of heel flap and knit 4 (5, 5, 6, 6) stitches from heel (Needle 3); without working, slip other 4 (5, 5, 6, 6) stitches onto Needle 1—34 (44, 50, 60, 62) stitches total; 10 (14, 16, 20, 20) stitches on Needles 1 and 3, and 14 (16, 18, 20, 22) stitches on Needle 2. Rounds begin at center of heel.

Work one round even.

Next round First needle: work to last three stitches, k2tog, k1; second needle: work across; third needle: k1, ssk, work to end—two stitches decreased.

Repeat the last two rounds 2 (5, 6, 9, 8) times more—28 (32, 36, 40, 44) stitches.

Work even in stripe pattern until foot measures 4 (6¼, 7½, 8¼, 9)" (10 [16, 19, 21, 23]cm) from back of heel, or 1 (1¼, 1½, 1¾, 2)" (2.5 [3, 4, 4.5, 5]cm) less than total desired foot length.

Cut CC and continue with MC only.

Jil's Tip
When slipping a stitch, slip it as if to purl; if you slip as if to knit, the stitch will twist and the fabric will tighten up.

Toe

Knit one round even.

Next round First needle: knit to last three stitches on needle, k2tog, k1; second needle: k1, ssk, knit to last three stitches, k2tog, k1; third needle: k1, ssk, knit to end.

Repeat the last two rounds until twelve stitches remain.

Knit to end of first needle, then cut yarn leaving a 12" (30.5cm) tail. Without working, place stitches from first and third needles on one needle—six stitches on each needle.

Graft Toe Stitches

Use the Kitchener stitch (page 108) to close the toe stitches. Cut the yarn and weave in ends.

LESSON 16

Jil's Tip
Never carry a color over more than three stitches because that will cause the gauge to tighten up.

How to Create Fair Isle

Fair Isle is a traditional style of knitting with many colors, but only two colors are worked in any one row. It is knit in stockinette stitch and the colors are carried along in the back of the work, but not for too long because long loose floats on the back can catch on fingers or jewelry. Try to carry your yarn evenly across the back to maintain an even tension: pulling the yarn too tightly will make the work pucker. The color pattern will be represented in a chart. It's a good idea to make a large practice swatch of Fair Isle before beginning your garment.

A Fair Isle pattern

Yarn carried across the back

How to Read a Color Chart

Because it is much easier to follow a chart than to read through instructions, colorwork patterns are often charted on square graph paper rather than written in words. The chart also shows you what the pattern will look like when it's finished—and even more so if the chart is done on knitter's graph paper, which is marked with squat rectangles in proportion to the shape of stitches rather than squares. On either graph paper, each square on a chart represents one stitch, and each row of squares represents one row of knitting. Charts are read from bottom to top, from right to left on the first row, from left to right on the second, and so on. If you are working in the round, all rows are read from right to left. On some charts different symbols represent different colors or stitches; on other charts squares are colored in.

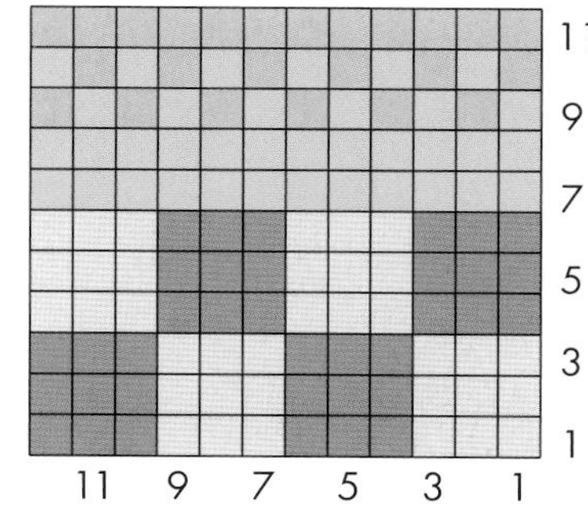

Color Key

- Lavender (A)
- Blue (B)
- Lt green (C)
- Aqua (D)

Color chart

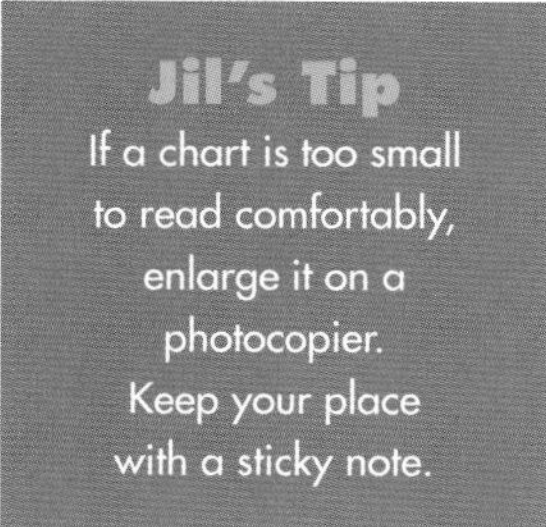

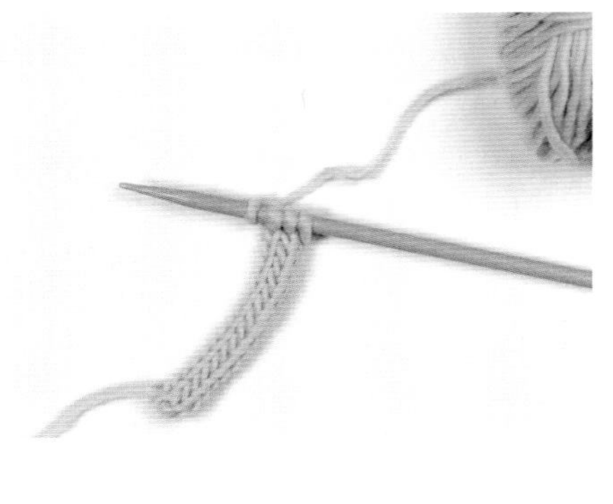

How to Make I-Cord

I-cord is a knitted cord made on double-pointed needles and usually used as a drawstring or tie.

1. Cast on three, four, or five stitches on a double-pointed needle.

2. With a second double-pointed needle, knit the stitches but do not turn the work.

3. Slide the knitting back to the right end of the needle, pull the working yarn tightly across the back of the stitches, and knit the next row, as shown.

4. Continue working rows until you have the length of cord you want.

I-cord

How to Make an I-Cord Bind-Off

Using an I-cord for a bind-off creates a seamless finish with a three-dimensional look. It's somewhat slow going, but well worth the effort. Working over a table really helps with this technique. Once you learn this sophisticated bind-off you'll be looking for new ways to use it!

1

2

1. Cast on four stitches on a double-pointed needle. Knit three stitches, and slip the last stitch knitwise into your garment needle.

2. Knit the first stitch on the garment together with the last stitch on the I-cord. Do not turn; slide the stitches to the right end of the needle and repeat until all stitches are bound off.

PROJECT:

cross country cap

Sample in photograph knit in Jil Eaton MinnowMerino (50g/77yds): #4757 Bluette (A), #4755 Cerise (B), #4735 Chartreuse (C) and #4785 Orangini (D). Knit by Stephanie Doben.

PROJECT:

cross country cap

A colorful unisex Fair Isle cap with a jaunty tassel looks challenging to make, but is easier than you might think because you knit with only two colors on any one row. The I-cord bind-off provides a smooth finish, and is less elastic than ribbing, keeping the hat in place effortlessly.

Skills

knitting on double-pointed needles ...page **106**
fair isle .... page **112**
i-cord bind-off .... page **114**
tassels .... page **89**

Sizes

- Baby (Toddler, Child, Adult Small, Adult Large)
- Finished circumference 15 (16¾, 18½, 20¼, 22)" (38 [42.5, 47, 51.5, 56]cm)

Materials

- 25 (30, 35, 40, 45) yards (23 [28, 32, 37, 42]m) worsted-weight yarn (4) in A, 35 (40, 45, 55, 60) yards (32 [37, 42, 51, 55]m) in B, 15 (20, 20, 25, 30) yards (14 [19, 19, 23, 28]m) in C, and 10 (10, 10, 10, 15) yards (9 [9, 9, 9, 14]m) in D
- One size 8 (5mm) circular needle, 16" (40.5cm) long, *or size needed to obtain gauge*
- One set of 5 size 8 (5mm) double-pointed needles
- Stitch marker
- Tapestry needle

Gauge

19 stitches and 24 rows = 4" (10cm) in stockinette stitch

Pattern Notes

- This cap is knit in the round from the top down.

Cap

Beginning with the I-cord at the top of the cap, with two double-pointed needles and D, cast on 4 stitches.

I-Cord

***Next row (RS)** With second double-pointed needle, k4. *Do not turn work.* Slide stitches to the other end of the needle, pull the yarn around the back of the stitches to work the next row from the right side; repeat from * for 3" (7.5cm).

Next row Increase one stitch in each stitch around—8 stitches.

Change to A.

Jil's Tip

Washing and blocking multi-colored knitting will even out the stitches.

Shape Crown

Divide the stitches evenly on four double-pointed needles (two stitches on each needle). Join and work in rounds of stockinette stitch (knit every round), place marker for beginning of rounds. Begin one-round stripes alternating B and A, AT THE SAME TIME, increase one stitch at the end of every needle on every round (four stitches increased every round) until there are 72 (80, 88, 96, 104) stitches, or 18 (20, 22, 24, 26) stitches on each needle.

Change to circular needle. Continuing one-round stripes, work 1 (1, 3, 1, 1) rounds even.

Sides

Continue to knit every round and work Rows 1–12 of Cap Color Chart once, then work rows 1–6 (1–6, 1–6, 1–12, 1–12) once more.

Change to C and knit one round. Cut yarn and leave stitches on needle.

I-Cord Bind-Off

With double-pointed needles and C, cast on 4 stitches.

Next row (RS) With second double-pointed needle, k4. Do not turn work. Slide stitches to the other end of the needle, and then pull the yarn around the back of the stitches to work the **next row** from the right side.

***Next row (RS)** Knit three stitches from I-cord, then knit the last stitch together with the first stitch from the circular needle through the back loops. Slide stitches to the other end of the needle, and then pull the yarn around the back of the stitches to work the **next row** from the right side. Repeat from * until all the stitches from the circular needle have been worked. Bind off four I-cord stitches. Sew the ends of the I-cord together.

Tassel

With B make a tassel (page 89). Tie a knot in the I-cord where it meets the top of the hat. Use the first strand to tie the tassel to the end of the I-cord.

> **Jil's Tip**
> For a uniform look, always carry a second color in the same way, either under or over the working yarn.

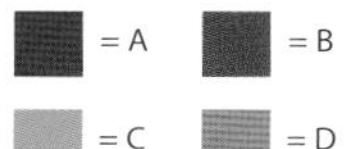

Cap Color Chart

LESSON 17

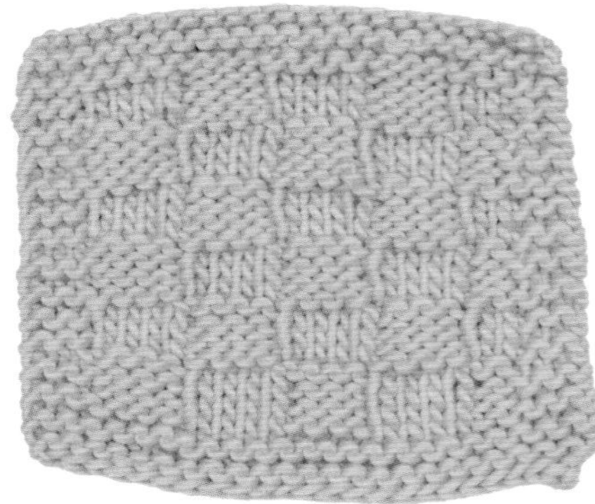

A checkerboard or basket-weave pattern

How to Knit Texture Patterns

Textures can be created in knitted fabric several ways: by alternating stitches, by working cables, and with three-dimensional work such as knit-in bobbles. Sometimes all of these methods are combined in one pattern; the popular fisherman knit sweater often uses a combination of all three textures.

The simplest way to create texture is by alternating groups of knit and purl stitches, used here to create a traditional basket-weave pattern.

DYE LOT

Yarn is dyed in batches and each batch is given a dye lot number. When buying yarn it's a good idea to buy enough of the same dye lot to complete your project. However, if you have to add a new ball of a different dye lot simply work every other row in alternating lots to make the slight change in color less noticeable.

PROJECT:
checkerboard jewels

Samples in photograph knit in Jil Eaton MinnowMerino (50g/77yds): #4795 Violette (A), #4779 Iris (B), #4735 Chartreuse (C) and #4731 Turquoise (D). Knit by Donna Gross, Nita Young, and Stephanie Doben.

PROJECT:
checkerboard jewels

A hat and mittens for children and a hat, scarf, and mittens for Mom are all knit in variations of a checkerboard pattern: a basket-weave hat, a checkerboard scarf, and mini checkered mittens. These QuickKnits™, in brightly colored jewel tones, are perfect for presents—in any combination. The mittens are knit on two needles and finished with a simple seam.

Skills

knit stitch .... page **32**
purl stitch .... page **46**
increase .... page **57**
decrease .... page **37**
sewing a seam .... page **37**
pompoms .... page **34**

Sizes

Hat

- Baby (Toddler, Child, Adult)
- Finished circumference 16½ (18, 19½, 21¼)" (42 [45.5, 49.5, 54]cm)

Mittens

- Child (Adult)

Scarf

- Finished size: 4¾" (12cm) wide by 40" (101.5cm) long

Gauge

20 stitches and 32 rows = 4" (10cm) in checkerboard patterns

Materials

- 70 (125, 170, 215) yards (65 [115, 160, 200]m) heavy worsted-weight yarn (4) in A for Hat, 80 (165) yards (75 [155]m) in B (C) for Mittens, and 165 yards (155m) in D for Scarf
- One pair size 7 (4.5mm) needles, *or size needed to obtain gauge*
- 2 stitch holders
- 2 stitch markers
- Tapestry needle

Hat

Stitch Pattern

Hat Checkerboard Pattern (multiple of 8 stitches +2)

Row 1 (RS) K5, *p4, k4; repeat from *, end p5.

Rows 2, 3 and 4 Knit the knit stitches and purl the purl stitches as they face you.

Row 5 P5, *k4, p4; repeat from *, end k5.

Rows 6, 7 and 8 as for Row 2.

Repeat Rows 1–8 for Hat Checkerboard Pattern.

Hat Band

With A, cast on 82 (90, 98, 106) stitches. Work in Hat Checkerboard Pattern for 3 (3, 3¼, 3½)" (7.5 [7.5, 8, 9]cm), end after working Row 4 or 8 of pattern.

Next row (RS) Purl row for turning ridge.

Next row Knit.

Continue in Hat Checkerboard Pattern for 3 (3, 3¼, 3½)" (7.5 [7.5, 8, 9]cm), end after working Row 4 or 8 of pattern.

Next row (RS) Purl row for turning ridge.

Next row Knit.

Shape Crown

Decrease row 1 (RS) K1, *k2tog, knit 16 (18, 20, 22), k2tog; repeat from *, end k1—74 (82, 90, 98) stitches.

Purl one row.

Decrease row 2 K1, *k2tog, knit 14 (16, 18, 20), k2tog; repeat from *, end k1—66 (74, 82, 90) stitches.

Purl one row.

Decrease row 3 K1, *k2tog, knit 12 (14, 16, 18), k2tog; repeat from *, end k1—58 (66, 74, 82) stitches.

Purl one row.

Decrease row 4 K1, *k2tog, knit 10 (12, 14, 16), k2tog; repeat from *, end k1—50 (58, 66, 74) stitches.

Purl one row.

Decrease row 5 K1, *k2tog, knit 8 (10, 12, 14), k2tog; repeat from *, end k1—42 (50, 58, 66) stitches.

Purl one row.

Decrease row 6 K1, *k2tog, knit 6 (8, 10, 12), k2tog; repeat from *, end k1—34 (42, 50, 58) stitches.

Purl one row.

Decrease row 7 K1, *k2tog, knit 4 (6, 8, 10), k2tog; repeat from *, end k1—26 (34, 42, 50) stitches.

Purl one row.

Decrease row 8 K1, *k2tog, knit 2 (4, 6, 8), k2tog; repeat from *, end k1—18 (26, 34, 42) stitches.

Purl one row.

Continue to work two stitches less between decreases every right-side row until ten stitches remain, end after working a right-side row.

Purl one row.

Next row K2tog across—5 stitches. Cut yarn, leaving long tail, and pull through remaining stitches. Use the tail to sew the back seam of the hat, reversing the seam over the last 3 (3, 3¼, 3½)" (7.5 [7.5, 8, 9]cm).

Fold up cuff at first turning ridge.

Finishing

Make a pompom (page 34) with Color A and use one strand of the tie to attach the pompom firmly to the top of the hat.

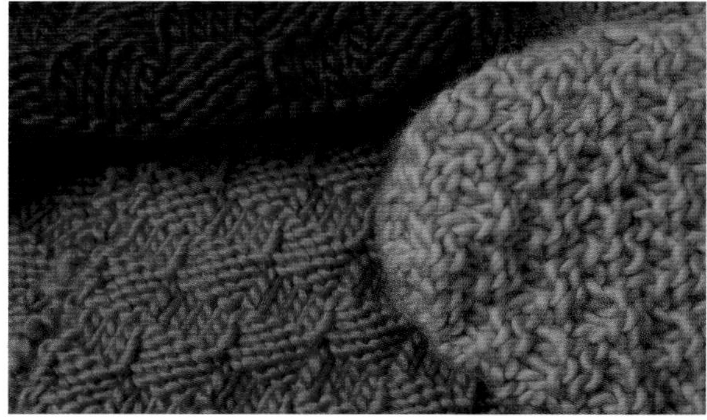

Mittens

Stitch Pattern

Mitten Checkerboard Pattern (multiple of 4 stitches)

Row 1 (RS) *K2, p2; repeat from * to end.

Row 2 Knit the knit stitches and purl the purl stitches as they face you.

Row 3 *P2, k2; rep from * to end.

Row 4 As for Row 2.

Repeat Rows 1–4 for Mitten Checkerboard Pattern.

Cuff

With B (C), cast on 32 (40) stitches. Work in Mitten Checkerboard Pattern until piece measures 1½ (2)" (4 [5]cm), ending after working Row 2 or 4 of pattern.

Thumb Gusset

Next row (RS) Working in pattern stitch, work 14 (18) stitches, place marker, k1f&b, work two stitches, k1f&b, place marker, work 14 (18) stitches—34 (42) stitches.

Next row Work to marker, slip marker, k1f&b, work to one stitch before next marker, k1f&b, slip marker, work to end, working new stitches into pattern.

Repeat last row 2 (4) more times—40 (52) stitches.

Divide for Hand and Thumb

Next row (RS) Work 14 (18) stitches to marker and place stitches on holder, drop marker, work 12 (16) thumb stitches, drop marker, work remaining 14 (18) stitches and place on another holder. Cut yarn.

Thumb

Next row (WS) Rejoin yarn and continue to work even in pattern on 12 (16) thumb stitches for 1½ (2)" (4 [5] cm), end after working a wrong-side row.

Next row (RS) K2tog across—6 (8) stitches.

Cut yarn and pull through remaining stitches.

Sew thumb seam.

Hand

Next row (WS) Rejoin yarn and work in Mitten Checkerboard Pattern over 14 (18) stitches from holder, pick up and knit four stitches across base of thumb, work 14 (18) stitches from other holder—32 (40) stitches.

Continue in pattern until piece measures 5½ (9)" (14 [22.5]cm), end after working Row 4 of pattern.

Next row (RS) *K2tog, p2tog; repeat from * to end—16 (20) stitches.

Next row *K1, p1; repeat from * to end.

Next row *K2tog, p2tog; repeat from * to end—8 (10) stitches.

Next row *K1, p1; repeat from * to end.

Next row *K2tog, p2tog; repeat from * to end—4 (5) stitches.

Cut yarn and pull through remaining stitches.

Sew side seam.

Scarf

Stitch Pattern

Scarf Checkerboard Pattern (multiple of 8 stitches)

Rows 1, 2, 3 and 4 *K4, p4; repeat from * to end.

Rows 5, 6, 7 and 8 *P4, k4; repeat from * to end.

Repeat Rows 1–8 for Scarf Checkerboard Pattern.

With D, cast on 24 stitches. Work in Scarf Checkerboard Pattern until piece measures 40" (101.5cm) from the beginning, end after working Row 3 or 7. Bind off stitches in pattern.

Weave in ends.

Jil's Tip

When picking up dropped stitches use a needle a few sizes smaller for an easier pick-up.

LESSON 18

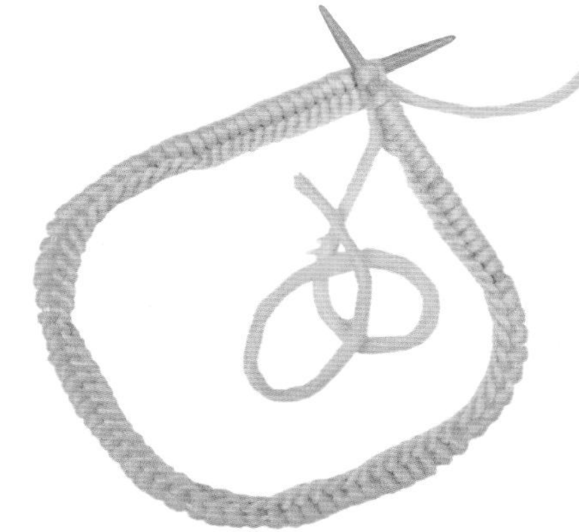

How to Knit in the Round

Knitting in the round allows you to make tube shapes with no seams. Each row is called a round. When you join cast-on stitches on a circular needle, it is important to keep the stitches straight, and not twisted. After you have knit the first few rows, you can identify the right and wrong sides of your stockinette knitting visually; the right side is smooth, and the wrong side has the purl bumps.

1. Distribute the cast-on stitches evenly around the needle, making sure all stitches face inside the circle.

2. Place a marker after the last stitch, and knit the first stitch on the other side of the needle, pulling tight to avoid a gap.

3. Continue to knit all rounds in this way, slipping the marker forward as you go.

How to Crochet a Chain Stitch

A crocheted chain, the foundation on which most crochet stitches are worked, can also be used by itself as a tie or a belt loop.

1. To make a chain, start with a slip knot (page 50) on the crochet hook. Wrap the yarn around the hook and pull the yarn through the loop. You have made one chain.

2. Repeat until the chain is the length you want.

How to Make Box Pleats

Pleats add dimension to a garment, and are best worked in stockinette stitch in a lighter weight wool so that they retain their shape. A box pleat is actually two pleats facing each other, one that folds to the left and the other to the right. Slip stitches—and sometimes purl stitches—are used to help define the folding areas.

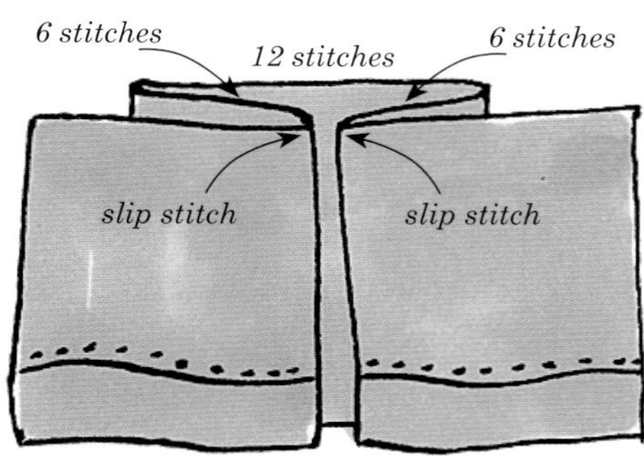

Six-stitch box pleat

1. Knit to where you want the pleat to be, then slip one, knit the number of stitches in the pleat including the folds, slip one, and then continue knitting.

2. If you are knitting back and forth, purl the second row. If you are knitting in the round knit the second row.

3. Repeat these two rows or rounds until you've reached the desired pleat length.

4. Bind off the pleat stitches and hold them in back, continuing to work on the correct number of stitches for the rest of the garment. Sew the pleats in place when finishing.

BETTER IN THE ROUND

To get a more accurate stitch count when knitting in the round, make your gauge swatch with double-pointed needles. After beginning to knit, use the yarn tail to sew a figure eight over the join of your circular knitting to create a smooth edge.

PROJECT:
dressy dress

Sample in photograph knit in Rowan Cashsoft DK (50g/142yds): #503 Mirage. Knit by Nita Young.

PROJECT:

dressy dress

A sleeveless party dress with an eyelet bodice, pleated skirt, and jaunty bow will steal the show, *sans doute*! A delicious confection for those darling girls in your life, the pleats add just the right touch of flirtiness.

Skills

stockinette stitch.................. page **46**
pleats .... page **124**
crochet chain stitch........... page **123**
three-needle bind-off.......... page **40**
i-cord bind-off .... page **114**

Sizes

- 6 (12, 18, 24) months
- Finished chest 17 (18, 19, 20½)" (43 [45.5, 48, 52] cm)
- Finished length (shoulder to hem) 13½ (14¾, 16, 17¼)" (34.5 [37.5, 40.5, 44]cm)

Materials

- 405 (465, 525, 595) yards (370 [425, 480, 545]m) DK weight yarn (3)
- One size 6 (4mm) circular needle, 26" (66cm) long, *or size needed to obtain gauge*
- One pair size 6 (4mm) needles
- 3 size 6 (4mm) double-pointed needles
- 4 stitch holders
- 2 stitch markers
- One size D-3 (3.25mm) crochet hook
- Tapestry needle
- One small button
- 1½ yards (1.4m) 1½"- (38mm)- wide wire-edge ribbon

Gauge

22 stitches and 30 rows = 4" (10cm) in stockinette stitch

Stitch Pattern

Eyelet Pattern (multiple of 4 stitches)

Row 1 (RS) *K2, yo, k2tog; repeat from * to marker.

Row 2 Purl.

Row 3 Knit.

Row 4 Purl.

Row 5 *Yo, k2tog, k2; repeat from * to marker.

Row 6 Purl.

Row 7 Knit.

Row 8 Purl.

Repeat Rows 1–8 for Eyelet Pattern.

Skirt

With circular needle, cast on 196 (204, 208, 216) stitches. Join, taking care not to twist stitches on needle. Place marker for beginning of rounds.

Next round Knit.

Next round Purl.

Repeat the last two rounds once more.

Make Pleats

Next round *K 23 (25, 26, 28), slip 1 knitwise, k 24, slip 1 knitwise; repeat from * around.

Next round Knit.

Repeat the last two rounds until piece measures 8 (9, 10, 11)" (20.5 [23, 25.5, 28]cm) from the beginning.

Next round *K 23 (25, 26, 28), bind off the next 26 stitches for box pleat; repeat from * around.

Next round Knit, leaving bound-off stitches for pleats at back of work—92 (100, 104, 112) stitches.

Next round Knit.

Front Bodice

Place first 46 (50, 52, 56) stitches on a holder for Back Bodice—46 (50, 52, 56) stitches for Front Bodice. Change to straight needles to work back and forth in rows.

Next row (RS) K 1 (1, 2, 2), place marker, work Row 1 of Eyelet Pattern over center 44 (48, 48, 52) stitches, place marker, k 1 (1, 2, 2).

Next row P 1 (1, 2, 2), slip marker, work row 2 of Eyelet Pattern over center 44 (48, 48, 52) stitches, slip marker, p 1 (1, 2, 2).

Keeping the first and last 1 (1, 2, 2) stitches in stockinette stitch and the center 44 (48, 48, 52) stitches in Eyelet Pattern, work even for 4 (4¼, 4½, 4¾)" (10 [11, 11.5, 12]cm), end after working a wrong-side row.

Shape Right Neck and Shoulder

Next row (RS) Work 18 (19, 20, 21), place remaining 28 (31, 32, 35) stitches on holder. Turn.

Next row (WS) Bind off three stitches, purl to end—15 (16, 17, 18) stitches.

Next row (RS) Work to last two stitches, k2tog.

Purl one row.

Repeat the last two rows twice more—12 (13, 14, 15) stitches.

Work even until Front Bodice measures 5½ (5¾, 6, 6¼)" (14 [14.5, 15, 16]cm), end after working a wrong-side row.

Place stitches on holder.

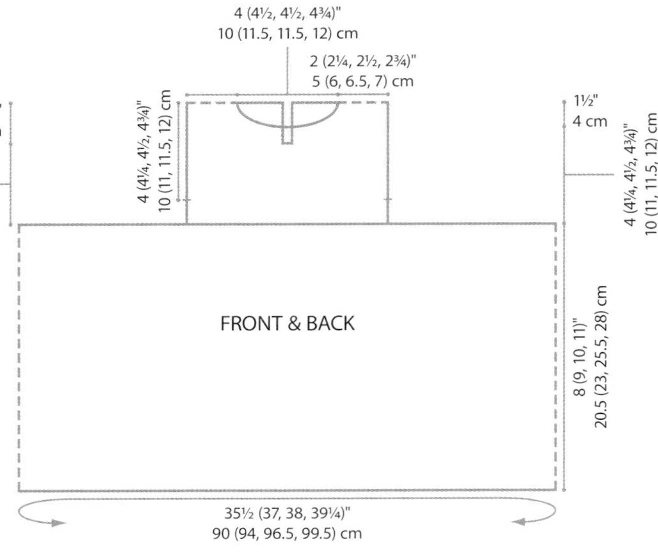

Shape Left Neck and Shoulder

With right side facing, place stitches on holder back to left needle, ready for a right-side row.

Next row (RS) Join yarn and bind off center 10 (12, 12, 14) stitches, work to end—18 (19, 20, 21) stitches.

Purl one row.

Next row (RS) Bind off 3 stitches, work to end—15 (16, 17, 18) stitches.

Purl one row.

Next row (RS) K2tog, work to end.

Purl one row.

Repeat the last two rows twice more—12 (13, 14, 15) stitches.

Work even until left neck measures same length as right neck to shoulder, end after working a wrong-side row. Place stitches on holder.

Back Bodice

With right side facing, place stitches on holder back to left needle, ready for a right-side row.

Work as Front Bodice, until Back Bodice measures 3½ (3¾, 4, 4¼)" (9 [9.5, 10, 11]cm) end after working a wrong-side row.

Right Neck Opening

Next row (RS) Work 22 (24, 25, 27) stitches, place remaining 24 (26, 27, 29) stitches on holder. Turn.

Work even until same length as Front Bodice to shoulder, end after working a wrong-side row.

Shape Right Shoulder

Next row (RS) K 12 (13, 14, 15) stitches and place these stitches on holder for right shoulder, bind off last 10 (11, 11, 12) stitches for right back neck.

> **Jil's Tip**
> When giving a hand-knit gift, include a card with fiber content, washing instructions, and a yard of the yarn for future mending.

Left Neck Opening

With right side facing, place stitches on holder back to left needle, ready for a right-side row.

Next row (RS) Join yarn and bind off center two stitches, work to end—22 (24, 25, 27) stitches.

Work even until same length as Front Bodice to shoulder, end after working a wrong-side row.

Shape Left Shoulder

Next row (RS) Bind off first 10 (11, 11, 12) stitches for left back neck, k 12 (13, 14, 15) stitches and place these stitches on holder for left shoulder,

Shoulder Seams

With right sides facing each other, and the front of garment facing you, place stitches of back and front left shoulders on two parallel double-pointed needles. Seam will be visible on wrong side of garment. Work three-needle bind-off (page 40) until all front shoulder stitches are bound off. Continue to bind off remaining stitches for left side of back neck. Cut yarn and pull end through loop. With back of garment facing you, work three-needle bind-off for right shoulder stitches. Continue to bind off remaining stitches for right side of back neck. Cut yarn and pull end through loop.

Finishing

Place markers on front and back 4 (4¼, 4½, 4¾)" (10 [11, 11.5, 12]cm) down from shoulder seams for armholes. Sew side bodice seams below markers. Center pleats over openings, fold evenly to inside of fabric, and sew in place.

I-cord neck edging

With double-pointed needles, cast on three stitches.

Next row (RS) K3. *Do not turn work. Slide stitches to the other end of the needle to work the **next row** from the right side.

Next row (RS) Knit two stitches from I-cord, then knit the last stitch together with the first bound-off stitch from the left back neck; repeat from * around neck.

Bind off three I-cord stitches. Do not cut yarn. Place the last loop on a crochet hook.

For button loop, chain 4, then slip stitch to I-cord. Cut yarn and pull through loop.

Sew on button opposite button loop.

I-cord armhole edging

With double-pointed needles, begin at side seam, and work around armhole as I-cord neck edging.

Bind off I-cord stitches.

Sew ends of I-cord together.

Belt loops (make 4)

With a crochet hook, chain for 1½" (4cm). Fasten off.

Sew belt loops at side seams, and on Back Bodice, 3" (7.5cm) from side seams.

Weave ribbon through loops and tie at back.

LESSON 19

Multistitch patterns

How to Work Multistitch Patterns

Multistitch patterns are worked in a single color and incorporate many different stitches, such as cable, seed stitch, rib, and popcorn. The possibilities are limitless for combining stitches, and the results are very beautiful. Patterns can be written out or shown in a chart. If you find written directions difficult to follow, it might help to make your own chart on knitting graph paper.

KNIT TO FIT

Never hesitate to adapt a pattern for your own shape. If you are high-waisted omit a few inches before the armhole begins; if you are low-waisted add a few inches of knitting. You can adjust the length of sleeves, too, just make sleeve adjustments above the elbow.

PROJECT:
latticework tank top

Sample in photograph knit in Blue Sky Alpacas Sport Weight (50g/110yds): #518 Scarlet. Knit by Joan Cassidy.

PROJECT:
latticework tank top

A tank top adorned with latticework lace and knit-in bobbles is a sophisticated design for city or country. The pattern stitch is challenging, but the garment is small and the results are quite elegant. Wear it in summer with jeans, or pair it with a velvet skirt for New Year's Eve.

Skills

knit stitch .... page **32**
purl stitch .... page **46**
increase .... page **57**
decrease .... page **64**
yarn over .... page **75**
bobbles .... page **102**
three-needle bind-off .... page **40**

Sizes

- XS (S, M, L)
- Finished bust 31½ (35, 38½, 42)" (80 [89, 97.5, 106.5]cm)
- Finished length 20¾ (22, 22¾, 23¼)" (52.5 [56, 57.5, 59]cm)

Materials

- 575 (680, 775, 860) yards (530 [625, 710, 790]m) sportweight yarn 
- One pair size 4 (3.5mm) needles, *or size needed to obtain gauge*
- 3 size 4 (3.5mm) double-pointed needles
- 6 stitch holders
- One size 4 (3.5mm) circular needle, 16" (40.5cm) long
- Stitch marker
- Tapestry needle

Gauge

24 stitches and 32 rows = 4" (10cm) in stockinette stitch

23 stitches and 38 rows = 4" (10cm) in Lattice Bobble Pattern

Pattern Notes

MB (make bobble) (K1, yo, k1, yo, k1) into same stitch, turn and p5, turn and k5, turn and p5, turn and ssk, k1, k2tog, turn and p3tog, turn and with yarn in back, slip bobble stitch onto right-hand needle.

Stitch Pattern

Lattice Bobble Pattern (multiple of 10 stitches +1)

Row 1 (RS) P1, *yo, ssk, p5, k2tog, yo, p1; repeat from * to end.

Row 2 K1, *k1, p1, k5, p1, k2; repeat from * to end.

Row 3 P1, *p1, yo, ssk, p3, k2tog, yo, p2; repeat from * to end.

Row 4 K1, *k2, p1, k3, p1, k3; repeat from * to end.

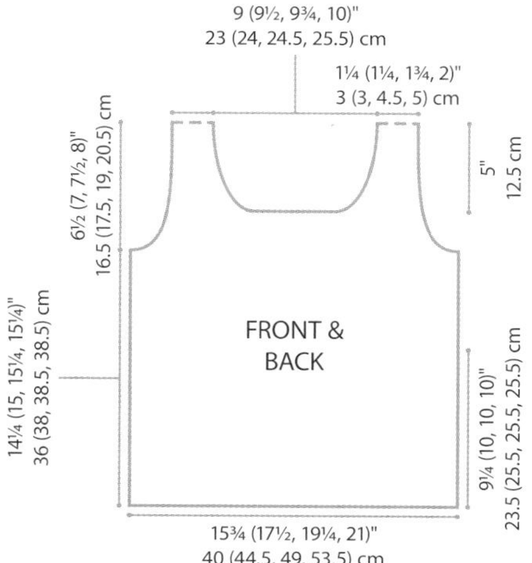

Row 5 P1, *p2, yo, ssk, p1, k2tog, yo, p3; repeat from * to end.

Row 6 K1, *k3, p1, k1, p1, k4; repeat from * to end.

Row 7 P1, *p3, yo, slip 2 knitwise, k1, p2sso, yo, p3, MB in next stitch; repeat from *, end p3, yo, slip 2 knitwise, k1, p2sso, yo, p4.

Row 8 K1, *k3, p3, k3, p1tbl into bobble stitch; repeat from *, end k3, p3, k4.

Row 9 P1, *p2, k2tog, yo, p1, yo, ssk, p3; repeat from * to end.

Row 10 K1, *k2, p1, k3, p1, k3; repeat from * to end.

Row 11 P1, *p1, k2tog, yo, p3, yo, ssk, p2; repeat from * to end.

Row 12 K1, *k1, p1, k5, p1, k2; repeat from * to end.

Row 13 P1, *k2tog, yo, p5, yo, ssk, p1; repeat from * to end.

Row 14 K1, *p1, k7, p1, k1; repeat from * to end.

Row 15 K2tog, *yo, p3, MB in next stitch, p3, yo, slip 2 knitwise, k1, p2sso; repeat from *, end yo, p3, MB, p3, yo, ssk.

Row 16 P1, *p1, k3, p1tbl into bobble stitch, k3, p2; repeat from * to end.

Repeat Rows 1-16 for Lattice Bobble Pattern.

Front

With straight needles, cast on 91 (101, 111, 121) stitches. Work in Lattice Bobble Pattern for 88 (96, 96, 96) rows; piece should measure approximately 9¼ (10, 10, 10)" (23.5 [25.5, 25.5, 25.5]cm) from the beginning.

Increase row (RS) Knit, increasing 4 (4, 5, 5) stitches evenly across—95 (105, 116, 126) stitches.

Beginning with a purl row, continue in stockinette stitch and work for 5 (5, 5¼, 5¼)" (12.5 [12.5, 13.5, 13.5] cm), end after working a wrong-side row.

Shape Armholes and Neck

Bind off 4 (5, 5, 6) stitches at the beginning of the next two rows, and then bind off 2 (3, 4, 5) stitches at the beginning of the next two rows—83 (89, 98, 104) stitches.

Decrease row (RS) K2, ssk, k to last four stitches, k2tog, k2.

Purl one row.

Repeat the last two rows 6 (7, 8, 9) times more. AT THE SAME TIME, when armhole measures 1½ (2, 2½, 3)" (4 [5, 6.5, 7.5]cm), end after working a wrong-side row.

Next row (RS) Continuing to shape armholes, work to center 25 (29, 30, 32) stitches, then place center 25 (29, 30, 32) stitches on a holder, join a second ball of yarn, work to end.

Next row (WS) With first ball of yarn, purl to end; with second ball of yarn, bind off four stitches, work to end.

Next row (RS) With first ball of yarn, work to end; with second ball of yarn, bind off four stitches, work to end.

Next row (WS) With first ball of yarn, purl to end; with second ball of yarn, bind off three stitches, work to end.

Next row (RS) With first ball of yarn, work to end; with second ball of yarn, bind off three stitches, work to end.

Purl one row.

Next row (RS) With first ball of yarn, work to last four stitches, ssk, k2; with second ball of yarn, k2, k2tog, work to end.

Rep last two rows six times more—8 (8, 11, 12) stitches each side.

Work even until armhole measures 6½ (7, 7½, 8)" (16.5 [17.5, 19, 20.5]cm), end after working a wrong-side row. Place stitches on separate holders.

Back

Work as for Front.

Shoulder Seams

With wrong sides facing each other, and front of sweater facing you, place stitches of back and front left shoulders on two parallel double-pointed needles. The seam will be visible on right side of the sweater. Work a three-needle bind-off (page 40). Cut the yarn and pull end through loop. Repeat for right shoulder.

Finishing

Sew side seams.

Neckband

With right side and circular needle, begin at right shoulder seam and pick up and knit 35 stitches along side of back neck, knit 25 (29, 30, 32) stitches from back neck holder, pick up and knit 35 stitches along other side of back neck; work in the same way along front neck—190 (198, 200, 204) stitches. Join and place marker for beginning of rounds.

Work around in k1, p1 rib for three rounds.

Bind off stitches in rib.

Armhole Bands

With right side facing and circular needle, begin at side seam and pick up and knit 106 (118, 126, 134) stitches evenly around armhole edge. Join and place marker for beginning of rounds.

Work around in k1, p1 rib for three rounds.

Bind off stitches in rib.

needle conversion chart

Metric (mm)	US	Old UK
2	0	14
2.25	1	13
2.5		
2.75	2	12
3		
3.25	3	10
3.5	4	
3.75	5	
4	6	8
4.5	7	7
5	8	6
5.5	9	5
6	10	4
6.5	10½	3
7		2
7.5		1
8	11	0
9	13	00
10	15	000

solutions to commonly asked questions

I've been writing my "Ask Jil" Q & A column in *Knit Simple* magazine for many years, and have found that some questions come up over and over again, year after year. Here are answers to those most commonly asked.

Can I substitute a different yarn for my project?

You can, but make sure the weight and gauge are the same, so your garment will have the correct drape and fit. Refer to the yarn weight chart on page 18.

Why do I need to do a gauge swatch?

Getting the correct gauge is the single most important step to successful knitting. A swatch takes a short time to make compared with the time you will spend knitting your garment, and getting the gauge insures you will have a perfect fit. Just do it, you'll be glad you did!

How do you change the gauge in a project?

This question has come up over and over again. Be careful not to go too far from the original gauge, and do make a gauge swatch for your new yarn. Then for every part of the instructions, beginning with the number of stitches to cast on, divide by the original gauge, which will give you the number of inches (centimeters). Then multiply the number of inches (centimeters) by the new gauge. For instance, if the original gauge is 4.5 stitches to the inch, and the new gauge is 4 stitches to the inch, then divide the cast-on of 100 stitches by 4.5, which equals 22.2 inches (56.4cm). Then multiply by 4, which equals 88.8, and round down to 88 inches (224cm). You will repeat this procedure throughout the pattern.

How do I fix a twisted stitch?

Beginners often twist a stitch when picking up a dropped stitch. You can correct this easily by knitting through the back loop of the stitch. Check your work often for mistakes because the sooner you notice them, the easier they'll be to fix.

Why does my knitting keep growing?

It's common for beginners to mistake a loop of the first stitch for another stitch. To prevent this, always keep your working yarn underneath the needle when taking it to the back to knit the first stitch.

It's difficult for me to pick up unraveled stitches. How can I make it easier?

You can run a needle a size smaller through the stitches first. Find the row you want to go back to, and run the needle under the first loop and over the second loop of each stitch across the row. Then unravel all the rows above.

Can I use a circular needle instead of regular needles?

Yes, just don't join your stitches—work back and forth as if you are working on straight needles. This is especially good for larger garments because it takes the weight off your wrists.

I want to try knitting socks, but am worried about casting on with the double-pointed needles. Any help?

You will be casting onto three needles. Working over a table, cast on the correct number of stitches on the first needle, plus one. Move that stitch to the second needle, cast on the correct number of stitches, plus one again. Move the extra stitch to the third needle, and finish casting on. Arrange the needles with the cast-on edge of the stitches facing the center. Place a marker after the last cast-on stitch. Begin knitting with your fourth needle, pulling the first two stitches on every row a bit tighter to prevent laddering.

When I do Fair Isle knitting my gauge tightens up. How do I prevent this from happening?

When carrying two or more colors in back of your work, never carry the yarn across more than three stitches. And try to avoid pulling the new yarn too tightly as you begin your next color.

about Jil

Educated in art at Skidmore College, Colby College, and the Graduate School of Design at Harvard University, Jil Eaton's career as a painter and graphic designer finally succumbed to her early fashion instincts. She designs, publishes, and distributes internationally an independent line of handknitting patterns under the MINNOWKNITS label; has an eponymous yarn line, Jil Eaton MinnowMerino, a super fine super-wash merino wool with a micron count almost as fine as cashmere; and a new line of one hundred percent fine cotton, Jil Eaton CottonTail. Jil Eaton's designs have a comfortable, chic silhouette, melding the traditional with the new, adapting everything in easy-to-knit projects with great attention to detail, fresh styling, and unusual colorways. Jil produces two pattern collections annually, designs for *Vogue Knitting International* and other publications, writes a feature column called "Ask Jil" in *Knit Simple*, and is busy with her next book. She lives in Maine with her husband, son, and Rexi-Martine, her Cockapoo.

The Team

Nina Fuller is the talent behind the camera, magically capturing all these charming models. A nationally acclaimed location and studio photographer, Nina has degrees from Silvermine College of Art and George Washington University in photography, painting, and printmaking. Location photography has been a creative focus for Nina, as well as photojournalism, as she trots from Great Britain to Australia on assignment for various publications, specializing in equine adventures. Her clients include L.L. Bean, Lands' End, *Horse & Hound*, the *Boston Globe* and Atlantic Records. She lives in Maine on a bucolic horse farm.

Isabel Smiles, an extraordinary designer as well as location stylist, moved to Maine years ago to create the world-renowned Pomegranate Inn Bed & Breakfast, a stunning small hotel in Portland, Maine. She continues to do select freelance styling, as well as prestigious private design commissions.

Stephanie Doben is my gifted technical pattern writer and editor, and a general knitting genius; she was also my amazing studio assistant for many years. She helps keep all the myriad balls in the air with calm aplomb and elegant intelligence. She is a delight to work with, *sans doubt*! Stephanie lives in Charleston with her husband and son.

Mark Dube is my talented new studio assistant who wears many hats. An avid and advanced knitter, he not only keeps me organized, he also problem solves and helps mastermind design and photo shoots, as well as working amazing Photoshop magic. He's also been known to scout a model or two!

The Knitters

My fabulous band of handknitters is the best on the planet! Knitting prototypes is always a tricky endeavor and knitting under sharp deadlines can be an ordeal, but these garments have been perfectly done. Bravo to **Nita Young**, **Pam Tessier**, **Stephanie Doben**, **Donna Gross**, **Lucinda Heller**, **Joan Cassidy**, **Mark Dube**, and **Peesh McCallahan**.

The Models

We shot this book at various locations, which included dragging equipment and lights from set to set, dodging capricious weather. But Nina worked her magic as always, enabling us to shoot young and old alike in perfect harmony.

Learn-to-Knit Scarf with Pompoms	Mary Elizabeth
Zany Puppetina	Marie Claire
Crew Sweater	Pete
Easy-as-Pie Pullover	Sarah
Seedling Pullover	Parker
Pooch Jacket	Buster
Duckie Baby Blanet	Sebastian
Bird's Eye Cardigan	Hudson
Garden Party Cardi	Destry
Big Fish Little Fishie	Spencer and Kennedy
La Petite Shrug	Keisha
Bobble Shawl	Rachel
Toasty Toes	Stephanie and Lucas, Mekdes
Cross Country Cap	Lily
Checkerboard Jewels	Briona and Davan
Dressy Dress	Sierra
Latticework Tank Top	Vanessa

acknowledgments

Merci Mille Fois!

This knitting compendium is my tenth book, and has been an adventure indeed! Designing all the projects, organizing them in a logical sequence, technical pattern writing, myriad knitting, propping, photography...it's all a fabulous challenge. I am once again so enormously grateful for the boundless talents and energy of everyone involved. Mark Dube is my multi-talented studio assistant, Nina Fuller takes all the gorgeous photography, Stephanie Doben is my ever-brilliant technical wizard who writes and edits the patterns and assists with everything else, Merle Hagelin is my genius stylist, Isabel Smiles is my design guru, and Joni Coniglio creates the wonderful knitting illustrations.

Betty Wong is my esteemed acquisitions editor, Linda Hetzer is my polished developmental editor, and Chi Ling Moy is my incredibly talented art director. Heartfelt thanks to everyone at Potter Craft for all your brilliant talents.

Thanks to the Black Parrot boutique (blackparrotmaine.blogspot.com) for lending us beautiful party fashions, and thanks to Isabel Smiles for sharing her wonderful abode for location photography. Thanks to both Aurora Provisions and the KnitWit Yarn Shop (www.yarnonthebrain.com) for location photography.

Thanks to my beautiful mother, Nancy Whipple Lord, for teaching me to knit at the age of four, and to my lovely late grandmother Flora Hall Whipple for teaching my mother to knit. And loving thanks to my wonderful and brilliant husband, David, and son, Alexander, for their ideas, unending patience, continual understanding, and support!

Thank you, thank you, everyone!

the knitting market

The delicious yarns and other products used in this book are available from the following distributors. You can always depend on these companies for yarns that are of the finest quality. Check their websites for shops in your area or for online retailers that carry their products.

Yarns

BLUE SKY ALPACAS, INC.
P.O. Box 88
Cedar, MN 55011
888-460-8862
www.blueskyalpacas.com

JIL EATON MinnowMerino
CLASSIC ELITE YARNS
122 Western Avenue
Lowell, MA 01851
978-453-2837
www.classiceliteyarns.com

KNIT ONE, CROCHET TOO, INC.
91 Tandberg Trail, Unit 6
Windham, ME 04062
207-892-9625
www.knitonecrochettoo.com

MANOS DEL URUGUAY
Fairmount Fibers Ltd.
915 N. 28th Street
Philadelphia, PA 19130
888-566-9970
www.fairmountfibers.com

ROWAN YARNS
Westminster Fibers, Inc.
5 Northern Boulevard
Amherst, NH 03031
603-459-2441
www.knitrowan.com

Needles

ADDI TURBOS
Skacel Collection, Inc.
224 SW 12th Street
Renton, WA 98055
206-255-3411
www.skacelknitting.com

CLASSIC ELITE YARNS
122 Western Avenue
Lowell, MA 01851
978-453-2837
www.classiceliteyarns.com

Buttons

CENTRAL YARN SHOP
569 Congress Street
Portland, ME 04101
866-297-7520
www.centralyarn.com

ZECCA
Handmade Fimo Buttons
223 Egremont Plain Rd, #215
North Egrement, MA 01252
413-528-0066
www.zecca.net

Dentist's Tool

Patternworks
Route 25
Center Harbor, NH 03226
800-723-9210
www.patternworks.com

Online Resources

Craft Yarn Council of America
www.yarnstandards.com/weight

index